ELDERS LIVING ALONE
Frailty and the Perception of Choice

ELDERS LIVING ALONE

Frailty and the Perception of Choice

Robert L. Rubinstein, Janet C. Kilbride,
and Sharon Nagy

ALDINE DE GRUYTER

New York

About the Authors

Robert L. Rubinstein is Senior Research Anthropologist and Associate Director of Research at the Philadelphia Geriatric Center. His research interests include social relations of older persons, environment and aging, and the lives of older men. He has done field research in the United States and in Vanuatu.

Janet C. Kilbride is a cross-cultural psychologist who has published in the area of sociocultural influences on cognitive and social development.

Sharon Nagy is a graduate student in Anthropology at the University of Pennsylvania.

Copyright © 1992 Walter de Gruyter, Inc., New York
All rights reserved. No part of this publication may be reproduced or transmitted in any form or by any means, electronic or mechanical, including photocopy, recording, or any information storage and retrieval system, without permission in writing from the publisher.

ALDINE DE GRUYTER
A division of Walter de Gruyter, Inc.
200 Saw Mill River Road
Hawthorne, New York 10532

The paper used in this publication meets the minimum requirements of American National Standard for Information Sciences—Permanence of Paper for Printed Library Materials, ANSI Z39.48–1984.

Library of Congress Cataloging-in-Publication Data
Rubinstein, Robert L.
    Elders Living Alone : frailty and the perception of choice /
Robert L. Rubinstein, Sharon Nagy, and Janet C. Kilbride.
        p. cm. — (Modern applications of social work)
    Includes bibliographical references and index.
    ISBN 0-202-36083-0 (alk. paper). — ISBN 0-202-36084-9 (pbk. :
alk. paper)
    1. Frail elderly—United States. 2. Living alone—United States.
3. Frail elderly—Home care—United States.   I. Nagy, Sharon.
II. Kilbride, Janet Capriotti.   III. Title.   IV. Series.
HQ1064.U5R815   1992
305.26—dc20   92-3053
                                                                     CIP

Manufactured in the United States of America

10 9 8 7 6 5 4 3 2 1

Contents

Acknowledgments

The material presented here derives from a project funded by the Commonwealth Fund Commission on Older People Living Alone. We are grateful to the Fund for its support of our work.

We have also been helped and supported by many people in undertaking our research and in writing this report.

We thank Karen Davis, Judy Kasper, and Lisa Berkman, who received awards at the same time as we, for their support and ongoing discussion. At the Geriatric Center we wish to thank M. Powell Lawton, Avalie Saperstein, and the staff at In-Home Services. Cindy Thomas and Rachel Gilman also helped with the interviews.

We have been helped by many people and social service institutions in Philadelphia and the surrounding counties; help has included advice, knowledge, and informant referrals. Because of issues of informant confidentiality, we cannot identify these centers or programs by name here. However, we do wish to acknowledge the degree and quality of help we received. Indeed, one underlying theme of this book is that the aging network in the Philadelphia area provides quality help and that, due to its consistent underfunding and the increasing number of frail elders, it is in danger of being completely overwhelmed if action is not forthcoming.

We also wish especially to acknowledge the help and support of our research informants. Their hard work and openness in responding to our questions has been greatly appreciated and it is our hope that, in some way, this work can contribute to a national policy on aging that increasingly recognizes the needs of people such as they. The population of elderly is growing as is the number of elderly who are frail or infirm. Their existence and the compelling nature of their needs suggest increased consideration of changes in national priorities.

Introduction

The material reported on in this book derives from a research project funded by the Commonwealth Fund Commission on Old People Living Alone, directed by Karen Davis. Our project, entitled "The Personal Surrounds of Frail Elders Living Alone: An Empirical Inquiry," was one of three research programs selected to examine how frail and functionally impaired older people who live alone manage against great odds to maintain themselves independently and, in some sense, successfully. Some of the questions that the projects were designed to address include the following: Who among severely impaired elderly people will be able to manage at home and avoid nursing home care? How do frail elders maintain themselves successfully outside nursing homes (Commonwealth Fund, n.d.)?

Our project on the personal surrounds of frail older people living alone was designed to focus on environmental factors that contribute to independence of these people and hence to their successful aging. Thus our central aim was to come to understand and to describe the role of intimate personal environments in aiding the independence and the successful aging of frail community-dwelling elderly living alone. Our general hypothesis was that active management of the environment is itself a source of well-being for frail elders living alone. In this book the significance of home to these frail elders will become abundantly clear.

Initially, we defined two environmental domains as of interest in our investigations. However, as we were to discover in our discussions with informants, not only were these domains viewed as significant but others also emerged.

The two domains that we initially defined as significant were *the personal surround* and *the home environment*. The personal surround is the intimate experiential zone extending around the body (and primarily centered in the home) that surrounds the person and represents the habitual active extension of the person into the world at large. Such a zone has been called a "second skin" or the "personal space" around the body. This is the zone of greatest articulation between the person and the

x   Introduction

immediate environment and experience of it. To use another type of social
science language, it is the zone of *personal praxis*. As it were, the older
person, like any person, extends not merely physically but also meaningfully into the immediate environment. There is thus a fine articulation
between the body and the personal surround.

The second domain is the home environment of frail elders. The home
environment is the next level or layer that surrounds the person and, as
such, it is the daily stage in which people live their lives. The home
environment is the domain in which daily routines and practices are
given personal meaning by reference to personal biography and personally emphasized cultural values. Within the home environment, the maintenance of a daily routine and the construction of a "day" can be
especially significant to older people who live alone. Similarly (as we will
discuss below in our brief review of the home environment) the person's
psychosocial relationship with the home environment may be complex.

A big difference between the personal surround and the home environment is that the personal surround is always with a person, but with
frailty the home may be manipulated so that portions are closed off or are
no longer accessible. Our findings strongly suggest that the older person
acts to slow or manage change by creating and maintaining a meaningful
home environment. Such management serves to improve control and, to
whatever degree possible, create a sense of personal well-being. As we
will also note, continuing in one's own home is a role that means independence, and especially so with frailty.

In our interviews on the meaning of the intimate environment, additional environmental components emerged as significant to our frail
informants. These were the social environment and neighborhood viewed
in terms of quality, history, and physical features. Initially, we did not
actively consider the possible direct effects of the social and neighborhood environments on the intimate environment—neither the personal
surround nor the home environment. While factors such as social support
were obviously important to people, our focus on the personal surround
did not include a focus on the roles of key supporters as maintainers of
the home environment. However, as the chapters below amply demonstrate, both social support and perceived neighborhood features greatly
influence environmental experiences of these frail elders living alone
within their homes. Thus an underlying theme of this book became the
severe diminution of neighborhood quality for some of the elders we
interviewed.

Another set of concerns influenced the development of our research.
There is perhaps a tendency to see frail elders, locked within their homes,
as rather passive and as prisoners of their illnesses. Whether or not this is
actually the case for each individual, it is certainly true, as we will discuss
below, that many of the frail elders we interviewed are victims of destruc-

tive social processes and events. However, one of the most important aspects of the environment is that it can be manipulated and representative, it can serve as a source of strength through its ability to carry meaning qualities and as a buffer to deleterious change. Thus under the influence of the work of Lawton (1980) and others who view the elder as proactive, it was our methodologic axiom to view our informants as constructors and creators, each as a manager of a self in a given environment. In attempting to conceptualize such proactivity, we identified three types of behavioral or ideological tasks, which we labeled *certainty, continuity, and cultural competence.*

Certainty refers to predictability, to maintaining life on a regular basis and with a regular rhythm, to routine, and to the reduction or rationalization of risk—that there should be no sudden drops in the quality of life, but the provision of adequate stimulation. In an important sense, certainty includes safety in the home, minimizing the possibility of falling, of fire or accident within the home. But it is more than this, and includes too the provision of certainty for those routines that contribute to the performance of minimum standards for selfhood. In our view, certainty was likely to be an important experiential goal of frail elders living alone, obtained in part through an adjustment of the home environment, particularly when threatened by disruptive physical conditions. Moreover, we felt that certainty was likely to be enhanced through processes such as *environmental centralization,* in which certain areas of the home are closed off from regular use and key functions are concentrated in one or more central areas.

Continuity refers to the maintenance of a stable or coherent sense of self despite decline, deleterious change, illness, or threat to self. Several chapters of this book deal with issues of biographical continuity and discontinuity. Environmentally, one way that continuity is maintained is symbolically through the utilization of key personal objects and possessions as well as through confidante relationships and the organization of memories.

Finally, *cultural competence* represents a concept that is nominally similar to, but in fact quite different from, the notion of environmental competence defined above. Initially, we viewed cultural competence as performative, deriving this from the anthropological notion that, in part, knowledge of what is appropriate in a given situation forms the basis of inclusion in a community. However, as a global idea this has not proved useful in actuality. It is more useful in tracking those behaviors that frail elders give up over time. In so doing, they give up one appropriate behavior, such as washing floors as part of home maintenance, to enable the continuation of another, such as washing clothes, given their diminished energies.

The sample of informants that we discuss in this book included 52 persons age 65 and older, most with numerous difficult health situations. All lived alone in Philadelphia and the surrounding suburbs. The city group lived mostly in small, owned row houses or rented apartments, often in bad neighborhoods; the suburban sample lived in a wide variety of circumstances. The details of the sample characteristics are given at various points throughout the text. The theme of city and suburban differences runs throughout this book. These persons are ethnically and situationally diverse, as we will show below.

Most informants were recruited with the help of local service and helper programs or centers from their present or former client lists. Many received state or federally funded help such as a visiting nurse or meals-on-wheels. In general, the interview format consisted of three sessions, each about one week apart, at the informant's convenience. A qualitative, open-ended, in-depth question format was used. Conversations were audiotaped and transcribed. Total interview time with most informants lasted a minimum of six hours, and was often more.

It should be noted too that all informant names are pseudonyms and appropriate details of cases have been disguised to preserve anonymity. Interviewer rapport with informants was usually quite good. Only a few informants did not complete all the interviews. In addition, informants answered a set of standardized questions about well-being, morale, social support, the home environment, and the like. Janet Kilbride (JCK) and Sharon Nagy (SN) carried out the bulk of the interviews; in most of the material we present below, the interviewer is indicated by the initials at the top of each case.

Because we wish to convey the feelings as well as the facts our informants shared with us, long sections of this book have been given over to verbatim accounts. In this way, we hope the reader will become intimately familiar with the life circumstances of several of our informants. While each is an individual, important similarities among all informants, as frail elders living alone, and their environments and language of choice can be discerned.

As a consequence of our interviews, our idea of the significance of the home environment has been amply confirmed, as our case materials will show. Additionally, our own discussion of the interview materials has compelled us to reframe our account of the informant interviews in terms of an issue that we had not initially considered: the political economy of choice. We focus on the choices these frail elders see themselves as having and why. In order to set the stage, we must first describe the cultural background to choice-making. And ultimately we will discuss the cultural and political climate that shapes choice-making.

I

CHOICE MAKING AS A CULTURAL IDEAL AND AS A BEHAVIOR

1

Choice, Independence, and Aging

The idea of independence is central to the American character and ethos. Independence represents the cultural sanctification of the individual through the ability to control one's personal affairs, legal rights, and moral responsibilities. A person usually enacts independence through action. In the American view, freedom is not only a basic political right, but it is also seen as a "natural" or innate personal trait or desire of individuals. The idea of independence is embodied in the person's ability to control the domain of personal affairs and choices. Even without significant resources, Americans believe, people still have their freedom.

In American culture, *choice* represents the natural environment, the fertile ground, as it were, of independence. Americans believe that you cannot have independence without choice, without options to choose from, or without making options. While choice represents the social or meaningful environment in which independence exists, choice also may be culturally viewed as independence operationalized. People enact their freedom through the making of choices. A lack of freedom reflects a lack of choice. And the choice *not* to choose is also seen as a choice, an act of mastery or control through rejection.

The environment of independence—the ability to make choices—is closely linked to the idea of *control*. Most clearly, people make choices about that over which they have control or in order to gain control. Thus what is controlled becomes a choice-rich environment. For example, if we own a home, a domain that we securely control culturally, legally, or physically, we are able to make a wide variety of choices about actions and conditions there. No one else can make these choices for us.

At the deepest level, however freedom is defined, it is a key element in our own folk theory of personhood. Americans believe that people need their freedoms to thrive, to prosper, to be. Choice making is diagnostic of personhood in American culture. People lose their sense of being and integrity as individuals when they are no longer able to choose for themselves. Civil rights laws have increasingly extended the domain of choice to groups of disenfranchised and disempowered people, even

3

when, as in the case of homeless mentally ill people, the choices made may be clearly deleterious or self-harming or as in other cases where the extension is more cosmetic than real.

Yet independence is dialogically and conceptually linked to the domain of the community. There is a social contract, we believe. Absolute freedom, while a valued and magnificent ideal or goal, is in fact limited because of the presence and potentially conflicting innate rights of others. Community values and needs act to constrain individual action. Individual action—the making of choices—should proceed with reference to community life, we believe. The debate between individual and community rights is one that is quite active in American society at the present time.

This is a book about the conditions of choice making for a sample of Americans who, like most others, subscribe at least ideologically to these values and ideas and whose sensibilities of personhood are also in part defined by them, but whose circumstances render choice making an issue with distinctive constraints and conditions. These are frail senior adults who live alone. For them, particular conditions affecting choice making are entailed by structural and contextual issues surrounding each of these statuses: being elderly, living alone and being "frail"—that is, having one or more health or functioning decrements that seriously affect the person's ability to carry out the expected and usual activities of daily living. While we will explore each of these statuses below, we will begin our analysis by expanding the discussion of independence and choice. Moreover, this book has been undertaken within the context of the recent interest in *successful aging* (Rowe and Kahn, 1987). This notion suggests that aging needs to be understood not necessarily from the perspective of the absence of illness, but rather through taking account of those circumstances that contribute to superior levels of function or activity, in spite of physical limitations.

The Realm of Choice and Independence

In American culture, independence is a cultural and personal goal. Our view of freedom is based on a perspective that sees the individual as a discrete unit and as competent and masterful. Dependency is to be avoided at all costs in the American view. The anthropologist Francis Hsu has described the American core value of self-reliance and its most persistent psychological expression, the fear of dependence (Hsu, 1961, cited in Clark, 1972). Margaret Clark, in a classic paper (1972), identified six modalities of dependency among older Americans: socioeconomic dependency; developmental dependency (period-specific helplessness during the life span); crises-contingent dependency; the dependency of nonreciprocal roles; neurotic dependency; and dependency as a culturally conditioned character trait.

Clark (1972, pp. 273–274) suggests that these six modalities define the aged in our society as dependent, but notes that "fortunately individuals are not bound by their cultures. Some are willing to relinquish lonely splendor in order to function as part of a larger society, even at the risk of being dubbed dependent" (p. 274). We certainly agree with this statement but note, too, that one of the most startling things about the 52 older frail individuals we interviewed is that they all saw themselves, in some important way, as independent and as continuing to be independent. This occurred despite objective circumstances that in some cases quite severely limited their abilities to be independent agents and despite varying degrees of dependency in all the senses described by Clark.

This must mean, then, that the notion of independence is not an absolute, but significantly that it can be tactically and situationally re-defined by the person. There are many examples in this book of just such redefinitions. However, it is unclear for the impaired elderly, as for any people, just what the limits to independence are, that is, at what point or in what situations a person no longer feels independent. Certainly, some such limiting situations come easily to mind, as, for example, nursing homes or other institutional settings. However, even in such settings, Independence may be defined relatively, not absolutely. People who are, say, merely physically impaired may feel themselves to be considerably more independent compared to someone with profound cognitive impairments.

The concept of independence may be viewed as having two parts. On the one hand, it is a "social thing": an absolute condition to which we all aspire as participants in American culture, a feeling that we intuitively know when we have it, or when we do not. It is part of our imagery, our advertising, and our official version of our history. On the other hand, independence represents a "key symbol" of American culture that is multivocal and that acts to condense in one word and one diffuse set of feelings a wide variety of events, affects, notions, expectations, and real-ities. Conceptually, ideas of independence may collect around a group of widely shared images of what independence is or means to people. Practically, one person's notion of his independence may be different from another's notion of her independence. Even though each person's view of independence may be defined with respect to the widely shared cultural concept of independence, each view is also defined with practical reference to the living situations each encounters.

Thus because of the malleability of this key symbol, the word and its attendant concept at its most global extend to include the possibility of wide differences in individual experiences.

Thus there must be some mechanism that is utilized by each individual to relate this wide definition of independence to personal experience of the same, whatever its specific content and limitations. There must be, too, some end point at which each person no longer considered herself or himself to be independent. The mechanism derives from the implicit sense of choice inherent in any situation. For example, as we will note below, many of our research informants clearly preferred their objectively wretched circumstances, but ones that included independence enacted through the governance of their own lives, to possible alternatives that included institutionalization or greater uncertainty.

Moreover, the mechanism of situational transformation is in part facilitated by the innate malleability or plasticity of the cultural symbol independence itself. It is socially and culturally necessary for this key symbol to have the characteristics of plasticity and extendibility, or else our society would cease to work, since independence, a central value, would need to be defined by individuals quantitatively in unequal amounts and specifically instead of relatively and as an attribute of most.

Further, because independence represents a collective or shared as well as a valued cultural idiom, individuals must be able to identify their disparate behaviors and distinctive interpretations of the life world as components of independence. This ability mediates the collectivity and the political economy of personhood in American culture, its emphasis on individualism and individual attainment, and a political climate that increasingly disheartens collectivism.

We suggest that the ability to make choices, even in grossly restricted circumstances, is subjectively diagnostic of a sense of independence. This includes the ability to choose rejection of negatively perceived options. Indeed, specific domains that are particularly evaluative of cultural notions of personhood, we feel, especially serve as the coin of choice and control. These include the control of personal time (the schedule and daily activities) and the control of personal space (the home environment and the personal surround). While these do not quite represent "the objectification (projection and externalization) of private emotions in a public idiom" (Obeyesekere, 1981, p. 77), they do represent the objectification of private experience in intersubjectively recognizable categories.

It is useful here to describe some responses to one question that we did ask informants in our study sample, recalling again that almost all were multiply impaired: What, in your view, is the most important aspect of being a person? This requested the infirm elders we interviewed to make an assessment, within their abilities to do so, of the single most important factor in their sense of who they are. Here are some responses.

Mr. John Rose, age 82, widowed: "To get around, to get up and get down. If you can get up in the morning, regardless of if you have a nickel, you might get something done, meet someone. Lots of people have money, but it does them no good, if they can't get up."

Miss Etta Cohen, age 82: "To have peace of mind . . . enough money to pay your bills with a little extra. And satisfaction with your own life."

Andrew Marks, age 72: "To be good, a good man. To have regards for others' rights."

Phoebe Deacon, age 85, widowed: "Independence. I wouldn't be able to go on the way I do without my independence. I'm glad I'm the way I am. . . . And, if people had more integrity, it would be a better world. Everybody lies, steals, nowadays."

Wanda James, age 84, widowed: "You have to be giving. You have to be warm and understanding. To be a person, other people have to understand you, and you them."

Annie Ford, age 90, widowed: "Being kind, considerate, to help out. . . . To get out. To help others if you can. To take care of yourself. To take care of your home."

Each of these responses refers to important notions of personhood— what it is to be a person—that significantly affects choice making, the array of decisions by each informant predicated upon their distinctive views of living. Above, we described the idea of *choice* as the setting or environment for independence. Without choice and control there is nothing to be independent about. In our view, choice itself is a multidimensional entity that consists of three components which we discuss here.

The first is *consciousness of choice* or the awareness that in a particular domain, or in any domain, a choice of some sort is a possibility. Not everyone has such realizations in all areas of their lives, and the genesis or denial of the consciousness of choice as a personal or social characteristic is itself an interesting and significant topic. How do we know or refuse to believe that there should be choices for us? While above we mentioned that choice is a diagnostic of the American ethos, or ideational system, careful investigation of the practical realm of choice shows that society denies both choice and the consciousness of choice to many people on the basis of gender, ethnicity, class, age, and other characteristics. While choice may be a part of the American ethos, one may safely argue that this ethos extends to within only certain areas and that we habitually do not think about choices in other key areas: things that are never thought, things that are "unthinkable," things that are not "for us." This denial or social circumscription of choice is undoubtedly a social, economic, and political process that is ultimately internalized by the individual.

Given consciousness of choice or the realization that choice itself is a possibility, the next element is *knowledge of choice*. If there may be options to choose from, then the question is, What choices do I have? Part of this component of choice appraisal is *adding and subtracting possibilities*, that is, learning about what is and is not realistically available. Again, the notion of what is realistically or practically choosable is the result in part of social practices that require the limitation of choices through the internalization that certain known choices are not "for me" for any number of reasons.

A final component is *the ability to act on available choices*. This, in our view, has a lot to do with successful aging. As we will note below, we define successful aging as a realistic knowledge of oneself, combined with a knowledge of choices and the ability to make them.

The above terms give the components of choice an unrealistically linear look, one that is probably not an accurate representation of how they actually work. For example, knowledge of choice may only come over time, or may never come; the drive to act on the range of choices may be an ever-present personality characteristic, or may be acted upon only in certain contexts, or again, not at all.

The crux of this model of choice making is in components that exist only in the best of all possible worlds, the world of theoretically unlimited choices. In reality, there are a large number of factors that limit choices among our study population. As we will discuss in Chapter 2, these include health limitations and economic constraints; the presence or lack of supportive others or appropriate guidance; lack of knowledge of choices; characteristics of neighborhood and home; pervasive or underlying fears; personality problems or lack of personal strengths; the effects of ageism—social discrimination against the aged—that are internalized by elders; and being overwhelmed, or the effects of multiple problems on individuals.

The reality of choice making then is very different from the picture that may be engendered by our theoretical discussion of components of choice making. There are real-world constraints to choice making. Despite the extent to which these could be beneficially changed, there are limits in that society is not necessarily fully committed to changing. Also, there is a scale of choices in operation for lifetime choice making. Under usual circumstances people are able to make choices about both big and little things: big decisions about the shape, form, conduct, and philosophy of life as well as the little things such as daily events. We argue below that when big decisions have already been made in life or are limited or become few, the domain of small decisions increases in importance.

It is important to remember that the ethos of independence, operationalized through choice making, does not dissipate, disappear, or diminish but continues to be germane and vital to those whose circumstances are constrained. People do not suddenly switch to some alternative framework of evaluating themselves or some alternative key symbols that give meaning to their experiences. However, as we argue in Chapter 3, an altered ethos of choice making does develop in circumstances in which choice making is situationally constrained. This altered ethos developed along two dimensions among the study sample.

The first aspect of the altered ethos of choice may be stated as follows. When one can no longer make some choices, due to various constraints, the personal value of the remaining choices may increase. Along with this, the number of areas to which choice-related attention and significance is given or areas that become choice-rich or "choiceful" may also increase. That is to say, independence and choice making remain important. However, the things that one can be independent or make choices about diminish, so what is left increases in significance, intensity, or complexity. Small choices become "writ large" and newly diagnostic of the basic ability to make choices, to be independent, to be a meaningful person.

The second aspect of the altered ethos of choice making for the study population is located in the experience of living alone. As we will describe below, the antecedents to present-day living alone by the study population are varied. Some have always followed a pattern of living alone throughout their lives while others have arrived at this state more recently and not necessarily by choice. Nevertheless, our interviews suggest that the structural realities in all situations of living alone, regardless of antecedents and predispositions, bring about an often unrecognized *culture of living alone*. In one sense, a culture is a way of solving problems of living. Small structural similarities within the context of a wider shared culture create communalities that must be addressed. At the very least among these are the following: the need to run and manage one's own life, including daily activities, meaningfully; the need to construct and keep a schedule; the need to connect with and maintain extradomiciliary social support and help; the need to pass the time; the need to maintain an identity and sense of biographic coherence that may once have included others as closer and more intimate. These needs may similarly serve to enhance the attention that frail elders living alone may pay to those domains of choice over which they do have some control.

It is thus important to note that this heightened sense of choice in diminished life space has biographical and historical antecedents. In the second part of this book, we explore socialization for choice making in later life by frail elders who live alone. We do not view socialization as a process that occurs only in early life. Rather, throughout the life course, any condition, state, or transition can have or lack a period of socialization. Further, these may not be immediately antecedent or directly unfolding. Some experiences early on in life may in fact speak to a person's present condition, although there may be a gap or interval of decades during which the experience had no particular valence. Like some other anthropologists who have analyzed the life course from the perspective of later life, we look to how these elders use the cognitive and symbolic raw material from their personal pasts to create continuity or bracket and mend experiential discontinuity. However, a major theme in this section is that choice making is part of personal continuity. We suggest too that the home functions to bracket episodes of discontinuity symbolically for some.

In Chapter 4, we examine the role of the home environment in choice making and the maintenance of independence, and we begin presenting extended case material from our interviews. We argue that when big choices are reduced, the domain of small choices increases in importance. We have also suggested that a transformation occurs of the cultural ideal of independence as a full-blown, activity-centered cultural symbol most directly germane to the most active persons. Specifically, for frail elders, this symbol is transformed into one that is most significantly enacted— one that can still be enacted and lived despite frailty—within the domain of personal space and personal time. Thus the home and the personal surround take on enlarged significance for frail elders.

Because the frail elders we interviewed by and large have lived in their homes for decades, these places have become meaningfully intertwined with their life experiences. The role of life history in affecting choice making is examined in Chapters 5 and 6. Integral to our analysis is the *biographic approach*, or the analytical approach that seeks explanation for current-day behaviors and adaptations in life events and patterns that have previously occurred or been established. Thus we ask the question, What is it about the lives of the informants in the study sample (as they described them to us) that may help us in understanding attitudes and abilities to create and make choices? In part, we examine the ways in which these individuals view themselves as independent agents, or not. But more importantly, we examine key transitions in the lives of these frail elders and the related themes of continuity and change.

A key notion here is what we may call *preparedness for transition*. Many later life transitions end up in diminishing the domains over which senior adults have control and can make choices. In a certain sense it may be easier or less disruptive to adapt to a new health condition when one has already had a chronic health condition over many years than it is to adapt suddenly. While adaptation can include a variety of different feelings and behaviors, it certainly includes the development of a new choice profile and the delimiting of areas of choice and lack of choice that one now has.

In the final section of this book, we explore the relationship among choice, control, and the notion of successful aging. It is fairly clear that some people age successfully while others do not. In a purely biological sense, there are many traits that may be considered markers of successful aging such as longevity and lack of illness. From cultural, social, or psychological perspectives, defining successful aging becomes more problematic. Aging, as a social process, includes decrements, transitions, and losses. Gerontologists have made several attempts to define "successful aging," apart from any biological or health component. In our view, and the view of others, successful aging can be built upon, yet be independent of, health and functional limitations: Frail elders *can* age successfully.

They do this by engaging in a balancing act. In our view, successful aging incorporates a realistic assessment of abilities and limits combined with the knowledge of choices and the ability to implement them through the control and manipulation of available resources. In this process, various components are balanced against one another; various standards are brought to bear by the person to evaluate or justify choices. However, as our case material develops, we raise the question of the underlying structural inequality in the opportunities provided to frail elders. While we do not intend our analysis to be reductionist, we are concerned with and critical of the lack of opportunities in the lives of so many of our vulnerable informants in the context of the degeneration of communities.

In Chapter 7 we list some factors that relate choice to successful aging. In the final chapter, we present some case studies of frail elders who we feel have aged successfully or unsuccessfully and we discuss the dialogic relationship of individual and community responsibility. We end at the larger issue that underlies this work: the relationship between individual action and community values.

It is important to note that a focus on successful aging that is oriented solely toward individual action or effort is inherently unfair and problematic. Above, we stated that while our culture holds up independence as a goal and a valued estate, limits to independence must be negotiated on the basis of community values and needs as well as personal and community resources. This then begs the question of what responsibility the community has to foster independence when it has fallen below a certain threshold: to ease adaptation, or to provide the resources over which individuals may make decisions? This is particularly acute at the present time as it concerns the increase in violence and degeneration of our nation's cities and problems in trustworthiness and national coherence.

Part of the ideological mystification of our own culture is that, in its public level of discourse, it generally sees the locus of such responsibilities as individual and not social. It is individuals who are "tragic" or "don't get it together" or who "don't rise to the occasion." Again, our American myth is that our society is an inherently fertile ground for choice making. Anyone, Americans believe, with hard work and faith, can "pull themselves up by their bootstraps" and "become somebody." Structural problems just do not exist or can be overcome, Americans believe. Despite the fact that civic nescience contributes to structural limits, there is a cultural failure to believe in the reality of some structural limitations. Since the locus of morality and striving is culturally seen as the individual, the dominant view sees society as having little real responsibility for providing opportunities for choices or control above a certain minimum. In the 1980s and 1990s the older view of society as a contract in commonwealth—between government and its people—has been replaced in part by a culturally minimalist view of government and a maximalist view of the individual or, at least, the individual who has already demonstrated success through action. Never has personhood been this much equated with what you own and what you have done; never has it been so commercialized; never has governmental action been more equated with dependency; never has the inherent dignity of personhood been more scorned.

Thus to pin successful aging solely to individual action treats only one current running in the sea of cultural meaning. It incorporates the reality that, culturally, people do in part view their ability to make choices as indicative of independence, well-being, and successful personhood. It neglects the reality that these choices and the very content of independence, while pristine as cultural symbols, are profoundly intermingled in the lives, contexts, choices, and sense of independence of others. It neglects the role of government as one provider of meaningful choice and as a means to overcome structural inequities and thus its role of providing what is basic to personal dignity and integrity.

Status Characteristics

A variety of criteria have informed the selection of informants for this study. In the remainder of this chapter we describe key aspects of the status characteristics of the study sample: old age, frailty, home environments, and living alone.

Old Age

It is well known that America's population is "graying" and that senior adults make up a larger percentage and number of the American population than ever before.

Americans are truly ambivalent about old age. The idea of old age still has many negative connotations. For example, while most of our informants in the study sample are chronologically "old," most do not feel or admit to themselves that they are old, in part because oldness has a pejorative connotation. Another American conception of old age is that it should be a "good" time for people, that people should experience "a good old age." In some ways old age is viewed in American cultural individualism as a time to reap the return on the investment in life of one's labors. There is a vague idea that seniors have earned authority and respect for their longevity and experience. This notion is an ideal, however, that reality does not often approach.

The idea of having a good old age has been taken up by social gerontologists in their concern with accounting for and measuring such formal constructs as "life satisfaction," "morale," and "well-being." Well-being and these other related terms are psychological constructs, or formal distillations of what senior adults are said to believe and feel about what is good and what makes for happiness in later life. In gerontology these constructs are represented by sets of questions that assess what people feel about themselves and the possible conditions (health or income, for example) that seem to affect the ways people feel about themselves. Because of their interest in discovering what contributes in whole or in part to better aging, defining and measuring these have preoccupied gerontologists for several decades. Significantly, there have generally been consistent findings concerning what life satisfaction in later life consists of.

First and foremost, the most important part of well-being that can be measured is good health and the lack of physical disability: The most substantial "piece" of well-being that can be measured is accounted for by feelings of positive health. Second are socioeconomic variables, primarily how well off people feel themselves to be economically. And interestingly, such factors as relative age, race, sex, employment status, marital status, availability of transportation, housing adequacy, and level of social activity, while individually accounting for some of the well-being pie, in fact only account for small pieces. Thus much of what "causes" well-being cannot be systematically identified and the largest known chunk is perception of health.

There is a difference between the objective assessment of health and what people feel about it subjectively. That is to say, the number or severity of particular health conditions does not necessarily translate into a given feeling about health nor into a given profile of well-being. Both the *life circumstances* and the *personal meaning and interpretation* of health are significant. These are part and parcel of the biographic approach, or the approach to understanding senior adults that seeks to enlighten present-day meanings and decisions with the biographical context within which elders have made these decisions.

For example, consider the situation of a now older person who has always had a chronic, but generally unobtrusive, health condition that has required constant, yet low-level monitoring over his adult life. Perhaps this has meant discontinuing or altering some activities as an adult. This older adult is well practiced at adapting to such circumstances. In contrast, consider the older person who has always been active as an adult but who has recently suffered a relatively serious medical condition, such as a heart attack, that requires an immediate change in behavior and in the way the person now thinks about herself and her capacities. A more radical kind of personal adaptation is required in the latter set of events. These two rather common profiles represent very different life circumstances that affect the experiencing of health in later life.

Further, health conditions must be personally evaluated by each individual so that they may understand the ways these limit choices and options and the degree to which trade-offs become a possibility. This evaluation process is part of the meaning of health or illness to each older person. Is a health problem "just like" some other problem that a person has faced and overcome earlier in life? How is it evaluated? What does it entail? Does it come at a time of deep personal losses or other negative life change? Can it be accepted within the larger context of life meaning? Does the older person have enough help from other people to face the illness if it is severe? These sorts of questions can only be interpreted and evaluated by each individual with respect to their own standards of personal adequacy. This is the balancing act we described above, the balancing of continuity and change in the various domains of life's restrictions and opportunities.

There has been a long-standing tendency to confuse old age with poor health. The cliche, often associated with senior adults, When you have your health, you have everything, is in effect the product of this sort of thinking. Behind this association is the full range of choices and possibilities that health commands: The domain of choice is large. With health problems comes a reduction in the domain of choice. But if, after the onset of a health problem, life once again reaches a steady state over a discernible and significant period of time, people usually adapt to the new plateau of choices.

We described above the conflict in cultural ideologies between viewing successful aging and its component, knowledgeable choice making, as solely the province of the aged individual or as existing in dialogue with opportunities provided by government and community. Health conditions in later life are also subject to an ideological conflict, eloquently described by Sharon Kaufman (1988) in an analysis of stroke rehabilitation and the negotiation of personal identity. There she contrasts two cultural ideologies of physical improvement. The first is the rehabilitation process, or the health care practitioners' goals for the patient (the medical model). This is the view of the outsider on what the patient *should* be doing. These are structured tasks, progressive performance of which measures progress in rehabilitative therapy. In contrast is recovery, a "nonspecific, diffuse goal" used by the patients themselves (the insiders), which implies movement toward "notions of normality, continuity and identity." These include "dimensions of the person that are not usually included in the medical model" (p. 84). The ideology of the medical specialists, the goal of which is to promote functional independence, she notes, reflects the widely shared American values of personal autonomy, the importance of action, and mastery of disease (p. 94). Patients are labeled "difficult" when they do not share or fail to demonstrate these values. However, as Kaufman notes, many people live with compromised versions of these values prior to the onset of stroke so that commencement of the rehabilitation process after years of not fully enacting these values is seen by patients as inappropriate or irrelevant. The personal meaning of health can only be understood with reference to a person's lifetime, experiences, and values.

Frailty

Frailty is a term that links objective health status with both objective and subjective personal efficacy and viability. Unfortunately, in its popular sense, the term conjures an image of someone who is physically weak and unable to do much, someone who is easily breakable. Technically, in social gerontology, the term *frailty* is meant solely as an indicator of physical health status or function and is used to describe a person who has a number or certain type of chronic illnesses as measured by a variety of formal scales. It is assumed, quite naturally, that frail elders are in part dependent on others for assistance with many tasks of everyday living such as cooking, bathing, shopping, and dressing. Persons who are frail may require long-term care, either at home or in a specialized setting such as a nursing home. A key question is thus, To what extent does frailty compromise independence or the ability to function at home quite as one likes and to make choices about how one will live?

A related, equally significant question concerns those psychological mechanisms and cultural abilities that aid independence or act as a deterrent to dependency. Because the notion of independence is so valued in our culture and the status of dependency so shunned, a great deal of policy and program effort has gone into helping frail elders continue to live independently at home. Yet the extent of such support is in fact comparatively limited. Most of what constitutes support for frail elders is informal, coming from self, family, neighbors, and friends and by adapting the lived environment.

The most common way that gerontologists have devised to measure frailty is by examining the person's ability to perform certain key tasks of everyday life. In general, these are divided into Activities of Daily Living (ADLs) and Instrumental Activities of Daily Living (IADLs). ADLs include such activities as bathing, dressing, using the toilet, continence of both bowel and bladder, getting in or out of bed or a chair, and feeding oneself, while IADLs include meal preparation, doing the laundry, doing heavy work, shopping for groceries, managing money and paying bills, taking medications, using the phone, doing light work, getting around outside the house, and going places beyond walking distance. Individuals can be "graded" along a continuum of number and type of ADLs and IADLs they can perform without help.

It is often assumed that most, if not all, senior adults who are frail—those who need significant help with ADLs and IADLs—live in nursing homes. This is far from the truth. In fact, at any one time, only about 5% of all people age 65 and older in the United States reside in nursing homes or long-term care facilities. It is estimated that of the 28.6 million persons age 65 and over in 1985, some 6.2 million to 6.5 million required some form of long-term care need, that is, help with ADLs and IADLs (U.S. General Accounting Office 1988). Of these more than 6 million frail elders, only about 20% lived in nursing homes in 1985. Of those in nursing homes, some 92% have deficiencies in one or more ADLs; 50% have deficiencies in five or six ADLs (p. 14). To put is another way, some one quarter of the 8 million or so older people who now live alone have some difficulty with at least one task of everyday living. Moreover, about 35% of elderly living alone who are poor have some difficulty with at least one task of daily living (Kasper, 1988, p. 54).

Most people who are frail and require some help with everyday activities live in their own homes in the wider community, by and large where they have always lived. Thus some 5 million senior adults, with various degrees of dependency, live at home, alone or with others. Two thirds of these are women. Some two thirds of the 5 million frail (dependent) elderly living in the community have one or more ADL deficiencies. Some 600,000 to 1 million of these elders are very dependent, with 5 or more ADL deficiencies (U.S. GAO, 1988).

It should be clear then that a large number of older adults with significant physical impairments continue to maintain homes in the community. The current population of some 6 million or so frail elders is the tip of an iceberg. It is estimated that there will be some 14.3 million dependent elderly in the year 2020 (U.S. GAO, 1988). This very large number of people will have profound social implications.

Who takes care of frail or "dependent" elderly? That is, who helps frail elders remain independent? Gerontologists have conceptualized the answer to this question in a variety of ways. Most important is the notion of *social support*, or the instrumental and emotional help provided by significant others to impaired elderly. Generally, such support has been divided into formal support, or those services, care, aid, and help provided through governmental, quasi-governmental, and other public means, and informal support, or that generally unpaid help provided by family, neighbors, and friends. A social support system, or the interacting aggregate of such helpers, may also be referred to as a helping network or a "natural helping network" insofar as the supporters are part of each person's larger total social network. In sum, key distinctions include that between formal and informal support and that between all the people you know—social network—and people who do things for you—social support.

Another key term germane to frail elders living in the community is *caregiver*. Most commonly this term is applied to the person or persons, usually a spouse or daughter, who is most directly involved in enabling an impaired elder to remain at home, although there is considerable variation in this usage (Barer and Johnson, 1990).

In conceptualizing social support, the presence of the term *caregiver* usually indicates a great severity of disorder since the impaired person is seen as requiring such a helper. Thus, generally, one is a caregiver to a severely impaired elder; the term is often used in conjunction with the presence of senile dementia or Alzheimer's disease. There is debate whether impaired elders continuing to reside in the community generally have one main caregiver or several. Nevertheless, it does seem to be the case that severity of cognitive (and perhaps physical) disabilities leads to a centralization of social support among a few key individuals and the diminution of the elder's general social network.

It is important to note that formal support figures very little in all this. For example, Liu, Manton, and Liu (1985) found that only some 5% of frail elders received all their daily care from formal services. Newman and Struyk (1990) found an association of formal caregiving with the risk of institutionalization, no doubt because those receiving such services are the sickest and neediest. In contrast, informal care represents the vast majority of all caregiving. Stone (1987), in an examination of those providing informal care, found that women made up more than 70% of informal caregivers and that nearly 30% of all caregivers were adult daughters.

The situation is more problematic for older people who live alone.

Kasper (1988) found that 73% of people age 70 and older who live alone manage with no help when some type of limitation or illness decreases their ability to perform daily tasks or activities. In comparison, 57% of couples and 38% of elders who live with others and who have some difficulty with daily activities receive no help. Of those elders living alone who need some help with daily activities, 17% receive unpaid help only, 3% get paid and unpaid help, and 7% rely on paid help only. For elderly who live with others, closer to 40% rely on unpaid help, such as informal caregiving, only (p. 54). Thus those frail elders who live alone usually have less rich social supports than other elders.

Home Environments

There is a direct and significant relationship between Independence as a cultural construct and home. While independence can be represented or enacted through a variety of means in American cultural belief (including purposeful behavior and activities), home ownership, home proprietorship, and the appropriation of personal space have had a long history as primary indicators of independence in American culture.

Rakoff (1977) has described the role of the home in American society as a polysemous cultural symbol that enables the mediation of a number of culturally based problems of meaning, particularly in respect to the actualization of individualism in community context. Family and community identity, personal status and success, permanence, nesting, personal safety, ownership, mastery, control and self-control issues of class and gender, all potentially contradictory, are involved here.

Further, regardless of individual history, the ethos that relates independence and home as cultural symbols developed in the context of the settlement of North America by Europeans and the florescence of a frontier ideology. Movement west was inexorably linked to the establishment of new homes. Each home ideologically recapitulated the nation-state; each home and its family represented an independent polity with lines of authority, rules and regulations, an established order and routine, and proper channels for legitimated emotions. It is not merely that Americans could move away when they could see smoke from the fire of the homestead in the next valley; it is that they could do so and once again reestablish what was culturally, for them, the "natural order" embodied in family, home, and productive labor, and the taming of nature.

This scenario also has occurred in cities. The movement outward from central cities took place in the context of expanding industries and the opening and establishment of new urban neighborhoods to house workers. Some informants in our study can recall moving to what is now a decrepit or decaying Philadelphia neighborhood when the housing stock was relatively new and feeling the sense of newness and the happiness of the new.

Whatever has happened historically and biographically to individuals, the equation of home ownership and home proprietorship with independence is still a vital and active one for those frail elders we interviewed. To have a home, to live in one's own home, to be in the home are very much part of a sense of personal coherence and continuing physical viability. This is true, in many instances, despite the presence of numerous objective housing deficiencies, decaying neighborhoods, and physical and health problems. We will discuss this topic in much more detail below. It is important to note, however, that because so many elders continue to reside where they have always lived, there has also been some attention, although not enough, to the phenomenon of "aging in place" and to the effects of standard community environments on senior adults with impairments.

Generally, though, the field of environment and aging has evolved with reference to specialized environments such as nursing homes or senior-only housing. A key concept in the environment and aging literature is the biopsychological notion of individual *competence*. Competence, a person-specific array of capabilities, can be assessed across physical, cognitive, behavioral, social, and psychological dimensions. Competence interacts with environmental *press* or the demand characteristics of the environment in its physical, behavioral, psychological, or social senses. Clearly, these notions have very important implications for how all environments may cause difficulties for individuals who are impaired in some way or additionally may be better designed to fit with and even help improve the capacities of impaired elders.

In contrast to supportive environments such as nursing homes and centers for assisted living, competence and press are negotiated independently by frail elders who live alone in environments rarely designed for the decrements of age and health. That is to say, older persons living in the community are the ones who make (or get help in making) environmental changes to fit what they see as their own capacities and proclivities. Or they just tough it out, with some or little help. This theme, that of the older person as the environmental designer, manager, or initiator, has been receiving increased attention in recent years in the environment and aging literature. In part this interest has come about in response to the notion that environments do not merely influence people who are themselves rather passive reactors (although this certainly is sometimes the case) but rather that environments and their users exist in interaction. Further, there has been increased interest in how the environment, at any level, be it a room, a home, a street, a neighborhood, carries meaning (see below). It is quite clear that, especially at the most intimate levels of room or home, the environment may be a fertile medium for the expression of personal and cultural meanings. But it is also clear from our informants that there is some variety in the consciousness that may adhere to such expression.

Thus, the home is, in and of itself, an expression of the core value of independence. It is an arena for the practical concerns of living and may further serve other purposes for older people and frail elderly in particular. It can be an enlarged zone of meaning within a reduced life space. As one of us has described elsewhere (Rubinstein, 1989), there appear to be three sorts of psychosocial processes that link the older person and the home environment. These have been labeled the sociocultural (or social centered), the person-centered, and the body-centered process.

The first of these, the social-centered process, concerns *ordering* the home environment on the basis of each person's view of sociocultural rules for domestic order. The significance of this may be particularly acute for some frail elders who themselves may have special difficulties in manipulating the environment, and those who live alone who must be solely responsible for their environments. Preserving the functions of rooms may be subjectively important, even though some may no longer be used due to health reasons. Further, certain rooms or spaces may lose their function due to physical or economic inability to repair structural defects such as a leaky skylight or roof, plumbing, or a falling ceiling. In contrast, the functionality of rooms may no longer be important and their functions mixed or altered, as health problems begin severely to limit what a person can accomplish at home.

The second psychosocial process that relates an older person to the home environment is called the person-centered process, and concerns the various ways that the person's life course, accomplishments, and sense of self are meaningfully represented in the home environment. While this has several parts, the key one is a radical form of personalization, labeled *embodiment*. This refers to a subjective merging of the individual and an environmental feature in which the boundaries between self and object may be blurred. Significant here is the role of an environmental feature, even the whole home itself, in propping up or corporeally aiding the elder when aspects of the self, particularly the physical self, may be deteriorating.

Third is the body-centered process, concerning the body in relation to the home environment. There are two components to this. First is *entexturing*, or fine tuning the extrabody environment to sensory modes in connection with daily routines. Older people, at home, may tailor their routines to facilitate a variety of sensory experiences, such as daydreaming or "feeling comfortable" in connection with the space and environmental stimuli that surround the body. Relaxing and reading the newspaper with the radio on in the background are examples of this. Related to this, and perhaps of particular concern to frail elders, is the process of *environmental centralization*, or the manipulation of the home environment to accommodate increasing physical and social limitations by concentrating living space in central zones. Frail elders may close off certain parts of their homes and undertake most of the business of living in a central location, such as a bed in a former dining room, a comfy chair by a table, or a kitchen table, that functions as part office, dining room, entertainment center, and communications center.

We will see many examples of these processes in the chapters that follow.

Living Alone

The trend toward living alone is one of the main demographic tendencies among the aged segment of the population. In 1980, more than 7 million Americans lived alone, representing some 30% of the elderly population (Rubinstein, 1985). Gender and age matter here. In 1960, 25% of older women lived alone; by 1980, this was 40%. In 1960, however, some 12% of older men lived alone, while in 1980, this figure was only 15%. And in 1980, about 35% of women age 65–74 lived alone, but more than 50% of women age 75 and older lived alone! Based on 1987 reports by the Census Bureau, Kasper (1988) found that 30% of the 25.2 million white elderly, 23% of the 900,000 Hispanic elderly, and 33% of the 2.3 million black elderly lived alone. After age 85, 45% of the 2.1 million white, 36% of the 170,000 black, and 30% of the 80,000 Hispanic elderly lived alone. The number of elderly people living alone will increase from 8.5 million in 1987 to 13.3 million in 2020, although the percentage of elderly living alone will not change. Women now represent 77% of the older people living alone; by 2020 this will increase to 85%.

Factors other than physical functioning must be considered in determining how frail elders live successfully in the community. Manton's (1988) study of a large sample of functionally impaired elderly over a two-year period found that even among those persons with five or six ADL limits, half were still living in the community two years after initial assessment, and only 15% had been institutionalized although living alone has always been considered a risk factor for nursing home placement. Kasper (1988) listed the following factors as those most likely to enable living alone: social support, sources of well-being in daily life, opportunities for personal control, and the physical environment.

It is important to note that there is considerable income inequality among the elderly and such inequality is disproportionately reflected among those elders who live alone. Crystal and Shea (1990) report that the worst off one fifth of elders receives 5.5% of the elderly's total resources, while the best off one fifth receives 46%! More than 58% of the worst off one fifth of elders live alone while some 15% of the best off one fifth live alone (Crystal and Shea, 1990)! To put it another way, 43% of old people who live alone are classed as poor or near-poor! Some 19% of old people who live alone are classed as poor, with an income of less than $104 per week. Some 24% of old people who live alone are classed as near-poor, with an income of between $104 and $156 a week. The 19% of older people living alone who are poor compares with the 4% of elderly couples and the 10% of those living with others who are poor. While it is expected that the poverty rate of married elderly and those living with others will decline in those years until 2020, the poverty rate (19%) for elderly living alone is *not* expected to decline.

Gender, relative age, and race are also factors. The percentage of poor and near-poor older men who live alone is expected to decline from about 38% in 1987 to about 6% in 2020; the percentage of poor and near-poor women living alone, however, will decline from about 45% to only about 38%. Similarly, the rate of poor and near-poor elderly living alone rises with age, so that 54% of those elderly living alone who are age 85 and older are poor or near-poor, while 37% of those age 65–74 who live alone have a similar economic circumstance. Again, these will be mostly women.

Twice as many elderly African-Americans and Hispanics are poor as are elderly whites: 43% of older blacks and other minorities, 35% of older Hispanics, and 16% of older whites who live alone are poor. Most income for poor and near-poor elders who live alone comes from Social Security exclusively, while income for other elders who live alone comes also from personal assets and pensions.

Certainly, living alone may be viewed in a variety of positive ways. With frailty, living alone may be a subjective marker of continuity and independence. People may continue to wish to live alone, to maintain continuity of life-style, to continue in a familiar environment, and so in all these subjective ways resist decline. Further, people may focus on the desire to continue to live alone, even in relatively wretched circumstances, in contrast to alternatives, such as institutionalization, that are culturally viewed as much worse and are haunting background alternatives to the choices these elders make. Such alternatives are seen as dehumanizing, as embodying a loss of control, as subjecting the person to the undesirable authority of someone else who is a stranger. Living alone may be viewed as an acceptable alternative, but clearly as an alternative to some other life-style, such as living with children. Some older people may wish that they could live with their children, but they may lack children—more than 20% of senior adults lack any living children—or they may view coresidence with them as an unfair restriction or burden on their children, or as an unfair restriction on their own privacy and independence.

Health status quite clearly affects the ability to live alone. The statistics presented by Kasper and cited above indicate that the vast majority of older people living alone manage with little or no help when faced with some type of health or functional limitation.

As we will illustrate below, living alone has many antecedents. The men and women we interviewed have either most always lived alone or had lived with a spouse or other family member until that person moved away or died. Variations in lifelong living patterns were wide. However, it is the structural circumstances of living alone that shape the similarity of this experience among the aged: The need to construct a schedule or a day, the need to manage slack time, to mix activity and inactivity optimally, to provide for social contact since none was in the home, to provide for personal comfort and safety, especially when ill, and to experience meals, sleep, hardship, and joys by oneself. The existential quality of "living alone" can be mitigated by the near presence of significant others. Having a close relative or a close friend nearby, next door, on the same street, is quite different from not having anyone of this sort close by.

Thus living alone must be seen as a mix of advantages and disadvantages (Fengler, Danigelis, and Little, 1983; Lawton, Moss, and Kleban, 1984). On the surface, it would appear that the negatives of living alone are magnified with poor health. The help, comfort, and safety that may be provided by others is not at hand. This, however, may be countered by what is gained through maintaining one's own household, even by oneself, and sometimes especially by oneself, in the community. Judged by the statements of the informants that we will describe below, what is most feared to be lost by ill health is independence.

2

Factors Limiting Choices among the Study Population

In Chapter 1 we discussed the idea of independence in American culture, how the realm of choice is the environment in which independence flourishes, and how making choices is, in part, the personal enactment of independence. American culture by and large operates under an overarching ideology of "freedom of choice." Freedom of choice is said to be available to all. This is, of course, a myth; freedom of choice is hardly available to large segments of the population who are constrained by limits to available choices. However, the possible realm of freedom of choice—the total range of things that one might theoretically choose from—is itself typified or symbolized by certain categories of choices. These include, for many, the choice to quit a job, to "pack up and move," to "do it myself," to "split for the Coast," to "make up my own mind," to recognize that "my time is my own." Interestingly, these are in part antithetical to an ethos of responsibility or community. We will have more to say about this below.

In this chapter we consider some structural constraints: a range of factors that most clearly limit the choices that our informants had. These include health limitations, low incomes, characteristics of the home environment and of the neighborhood, and fear. We introduce a good deal of case material and begin to make the reader familiar with the lives of our informants.

Certainly, choices have other limits that are significant. These include the lack of supportive others or appropriate guidance, the lack of the knowledge of choices, and the effects of ageism. These are addressed at different points in the text. It is interesting to note that the factors we discuss vary from those that are almost purely negative in effect, such as health problems, low income, or lack of knowledge, to those that are more complex and not necessarily limitations per se, such as investment in home and neighborhood.

Health Problems

In 1980 26% of American elders rated their health as excellent, 37% as good, 25% as fair, and 12% as poor. Some 40% were limited in activity and the average number of illness conditions for Americans age 65 and over was 4.4 (Rice, 1989). These figures are in some ways significantly different from the health of elders in most big cities and the health profile of the elders in our interview sample.

Some figures from a recent report by the Philadelphia Health Management Corporation (1990) analyzing a survey of elder health needs are startling and disquieting. There are about 250,000 persons aged 65 or older in Philadelphia, or some 16% of the population. Some 44% of these live alone. Of all elders, nearly 38% believe their health to be fair or poor; 21% have ADL limitations; 44% have IADL limitations; 8% have no regular source of health care; 8% have few or no social supports. One third of elders in Philadelphia have individual or spousal incomes below the poverty line, but this is true for 40% of those who live alone. Some 9,300 elders (or 3.7%) in Philadelphia are currently receiving home health services, but a nearly equal number say they need them and are not receiving them. There is no reason to believe that these figures are radically different from those in other major cities. Our research sample was different from the national picture. Ten percent (vs. 26%) rated their health as excellent, 35% (vs. 37%) as good, 42% (vs. 25%) as fair, and 13% (vs. 12%) as poor. Our informants were much less likely to rate their health as excellent and much more likely to rate their health as only fair.

The average number of health conditions in our sample per person, as measured by a 23-item checklist, was 5.5, but elimination of the 10 informants with the fewest symptoms as measured on the checklist significantly increases this average. Telling, too, were the frequencies of those who felt their health problems got in the way of doing the things they wanted a great deal (65%), a little (25%), or not at all (10%). Further, large percentages of the sample suffered from specific deleterious conditions. Twenty (of 52) had hypertension, 24 had heart problems, 17 had circulation problems, 45 had arthritis, 17 had trouble sleeping, and 26 suffered from nervousness and tension. Responses to a checklist of 22 health conditions experienced in the past year ranged from 1 to 11 per person; informants additionally named several other problems that were not covered by the checklist. Further, 2 of the subjects were double amputees and 1 was a single amputee. One informant was blind; 9 were partially blind, and 4 others rated their eyesight as poor. Twenty-six used canes, 14 walkers, 6 wheelchairs. Eighteen received homemaker services, 4 a visiting nurse, and 18 meals-on-wheels. Most were hooked up with the formal senior social service network. Thirty-four of 52 felt their overall health was not as good as three years ago, 13 felt it was about the same, and only 5 felt it was better. All in all, this was not a healthy group of people.

We asked some informants whether they thought of themselves as "sick" or "frail." Of the 39 from whom we obtained responses, 31% answered yes. We asked 40 of the 52 whether they felt their frailty or illnesses were controlling their lives; 17 replied yes, and 12 said "somewhat" or "to a degree." Only 11 replied no. Thus some 72% perceived their illness as in some way controlling their lives.

What do these figures mean for the individuals we interviewed? The following case examples will illustrate a radical example of how poor health affects choice making.

James Devlin (RLR)

Asked to name his medical problems, Mr. Devlin, age 70, listed his amputations, diabetes, and chronic stomach difficulties. Diabetes had led to amputation of both legs within the previous five years. These were high cuts that made it very difficult for him to maneuver in his wheelchair, from which he had a fear of falling, and from there to his bed. His health was, by his own admission, poor. Despite diabetes, he drank beer on the occasions of his interviews. He also suffered from chronic stomach difficulties, including diarrhea, that prevented him from going too far from his home. Not that he was able to get out of his home much anyway. Asked about outside activities that he had performed in the last year, he noted that he had "never" gone to a senior center, church, clubs, movies, or a baseball game, played cards, eaten out, visited a friend or had a visitor overnight, or done volunteer work. Confined to his wheelchair, his realm was his home and the small porch at the front of his row house. Because his row house was so narrow, it did not provide enough space at the front for a wheelchair ramp to be pitched at the proper gradient. As a result, it was difficult for him to maneuver down the homemade ramp at the front of his house without help. Further, the path at the back of his house that led down the alleyway that separated two strips of row houses was very narrow, not paved, and covered with boulders that made it difficult to roll his wheelchair down.

His health needs were severe, he felt, and yet it required all his efforts to prepare himself for a trip to his doctor, whom he saw irregularly, and who did not seem to make house calls. With his mobility problems, Mr. Devlin needed special transport to get to his doctor's office; so, once he arranged his appointment with the doctor, he was dependent on a private van service that transported the wheelchair-bound. This was often late and on occasion did not show up.

Mr. Devlin was divorced and estranged from his children. His wife had abandoned him earlier in life and taken them with her. He now lived in a small home in an area that was undergoing considerable change, as it moved from a predominantly working-class neighborhood to a poor one. Its infrastructure of small factories had become increasingly marginal and underutilized, then eventually abandoned and blighted. In contrast, strips of row houses were more varied in their occupancy and maintenance. Mr. Devlin's row house consisted of three stories; he lived on the ground floor and rented out the rooms in the upper floors. Lacking family, Mr. Devlin traded with a younger boarder for personal services in lieu of rent and also had one friend, a man some ten years older, who came by twice a week to help with errands.

Mr. Devlin was involved in the social service network, and "had" a social worker who could at times help with medical appointments and other needs; however, the caseload of the social worker was so large that more intimate support was difficult. He noted that he was lonely sometimes, but especially in winter when bad weather prevented him from wheeling himself out onto his porch and watching the passing parade of people. He read a great deal and the television was constantly on.

Given a choice of four possible explanations for why he lived alone, Mr. Devlin chose "because you prefer to be independent," not that there was no other place to live, nor because he enjoyed being alone, nor because there was no one to come to live with him. While he did not especially enjoy living alone, the other possible explanations were also true for him. He contrasted his present-day circumstances with the independence and mobility he had had as a younger man; he was depressed about his current state of affairs. Yet he still viewed himself as independent in contrast to other possibilities and life-styles he could foresee. Despite his health problems and the degree to which he at times felt victimized by the medical system, he still viewed himself as innately independent and able to make some important choices in life.

Income

As noted above, many older people have sufficient enough income, from a combination of Social Security, pensions, savings, and investments, to live out their lives without significant financial hardship. Those most vulnerable to poverty are elderly widows, the very old, and members of minority groups. This represents some two in every five elders living alone. And, in addition, half of the people over age 85 living alone are poor.

For those who do not have enough money to attain a minimum level of comfort or make necessary adjustments in their living conditions, declining health, shrinking social networks and reduced physical mobility can make old age very difficult. Those who until now have lived with little financial hardship can easily be reduced to severe poverty by one illness or major expense.

The elders we interviewed had an average annual income between $6,000 and $7,999 (that is, between $115 and $153 per week). About 60% of our sample fell into the poor or near-poor categories. Social security was the major source of income for our sample; none worked, although a few had additional pensions, investments, or savings.

The following summarizes the annual incomes of our sample:

Number of persons	Annual income
5	< $ 4,500
11	4,500– 5,999
10	6,000– 7,999
8	8,000– 9,999
4	10,000–14,999
4	15,000–19,999
1	20,000–29,999
0	30,000–39,999
0	40,000–49,999
1	> 50,000

(Total sample, 52, number responding, 44, no response, 8.)

The most important aspects of financial stability in the minds of our informants are home ownership and the ability to work for pay. Most worked at one time, but no longer do so, because of health problems and lack of opportunity. Amazingly, some say they feel that they would like to be working, at least part-time, despite their own health problems! Retirement was not always desired and signaled the loss of one domain in which they could assert their independence.

One reason home owning is very important to many of our informants is that it is a source of financial security. Most of our informants, like most older Philadelphians, own their own homes. Each home was a place to which they belonged, a place from which they would not be asked to move because of failure to pay rent. As we discuss later, these home owners are sometimes willing to live in inferior conditions in exchange

for the certainty afforded them by owning their own home and controlling their own space and time use. Many informants gained comfort from
knowing that they would always have a roof over their heads, even if it
did leak a little or was in a crime-ridden neighborhood.

Mr. John Peters, for example, at age 67, still lives in the home his family
moved to when he was 17 years old. He explained that financially,
"owning a home is like having a little job." If he did not own it, he would
somehow have to come up with rent money. "The best thing about living
here is the fact that it is mine. I have always had a fear of going broke.
And, it is getting worse as I get older, when I have less time to go broke in
. . . I think my home gives me a feeling of safety. As long as I've got it. I
think that could be another worriment. I dread not just going in a home
but ending up being in a shelter or, God forbid, a street person."

These elders rarely have any means by which they can increase their
incomes. None of them are currently employed. Several informants expressed a desire to work part-time. For example, one of our younger
informants, 65-year-old old Thelma Miles, believed that she was still
young enough and able enough to be working. Mrs. Miles lives in her
own row house in North Philadelphia, a poor and largely black area of
town. She had spent the majority of her working years working as a
housekeeper and nanny for a well-to-do family with whom she still keeps
in touch. In fact, our interviews had to be postponed for several weeks
while she went on a vacation to visit this family in Florida. She keeps
photos of the children in photo albums in her dining room. After Mrs.
Miles's services were no longer needed by the family, she continued in
domestic service. Her last job before retirement was as a chambermaid in
a retirement home.

She mentioned several times during our interviews that she felt she
was still capable of doing this work part-time, despite requiring assistance in caring for her own home. Mrs. Miles has a homemaker who
comes twice weekly; she also receives meals-on-wheels, and her son
assists with all the other ADLs. It is not so much that Mrs. Miles is
denying her physical limitations as that she desires a role that allows her
to be of assistance to others, while at the same time bringing in some
additional income. Mrs. Miles takes great pride in recounting stories
about the children she helped raise and the residents she assisted in the
retirement home. Despite her limited mobility caused by severe arthritis
in the spine and legs, Mrs. Miles is indeed capable of holding a job. She is
both intelligent and efficient.

Dorothy Douglas, age 72, suffers from heart disease and severe asthma.
Mrs. Douglas presents herself as a very strong, stubborn, somewhat
masculine woman, and claims it was her unhappy, abusive marriage that
"hardened" her. She stated that since separating from her husband 10

years ago, she has lived "the happiest years of my life." She has been able to divert all the skills and qualities she was forced to develop in her marriage to more productive and creative endeavors. Mrs. Douglas is now very active in a local senior citizen center and in a network of senior activities. The past few weeks she has been substituting in the lunchroom for the cashier, who has been out sick. All of these are on a volunteer basis, within the limits dictated by her health conditions. She is planning to ask the center's director to give her this job permanently because it is a paid position. Aware of the value of her work, Mrs. Douglas would like to be compensated for it.

Related to the issue of supplementing one's income is the problem of obtaining the economic benefits to which one is entitled. Above, we described knowledge of choice as one in a three-part system of choice making that includes consciousness of choice, knowledge of choice, and the ability to act on available choices. Frail elders present unique problems that complicate this; consciousness, knowledge, and enactment may be precluded by preoccupation with or complications of health and functioning problems. For example, physical and social limitations prevent some from applying for or collecting certain benefits. One woman in our sample was eligible for food stamps and had indeed used them for a number of years. However, now that she can no longer stand for long periods of time or walk far, she is unable to go to pick up her food stamps. Unfortunately the only person she has whom she could authorize to pick them up for her is her son, who now works two jobs and so is unable to get away during business hours.

The forms required to apply for utility rebates, public housing assistance, and other benefits can often be confusing. And dealing with agencies by phone can be just as bewildering. Several of the people interviewed for our research in fact asked the interviewers for assistance filling out forms that they could either not understand, not read because of failing eyesight, or not fill out because of arthritic hands. One 85-year-old woman with Parkinson's disease had been receiving mail from a variety of social service agencies informing her of the several services to which she was entitled. These letters were piling up on her dining room table. She asked for assistance interpreting the bureaucratic jargon in a few of them. One that had been sitting there for over a month informed her of a transportation and companion service for shopping and doctor visits. She said she had called the number given for more information several times but kept getting a recording that she could not hear very well. In the meantime, she has been paying neighbors to shop for her.

On a limited, fixed, shamefully low income with few options for supplementing this income, it is not surprising that financial considerations influence the full range of choices faced by these frail elders. Housing and moving costs are central in decisions about moving. Miss Alberta stated frankly, "I stay here because I don't pay no gas or no electric here."

Home repairs are sometimes postponed indefinitely. When Mr. Peters was asked if there were any repairs he would like done in his home, he answered, "Oh yes. I could sit here and dream. But I wouldn't want to spend money. I think it would be throwing good money after bad. I'll put up with it for the short time. I feel that eventually I will leave it one way or another."

A public housing resident, Mrs. Hines is concerned about her future. She has no savings and receives $357 a month from Social Security. She noted, "A person in my situation with no savings. If I couldn't care for myself or this place, what would happen to me? There's no more Byberry [a state hospital that recently closed] to put people in. I often think of what will happen to me."

Medical expenses vie with home costs for the most important financial concerns of frail elders. In addition to those medical bills not covered by Medicare, these individuals must bear the costs of prescription and non-prescription medication and health care aids and equipment.

Mrs. Edith Amabel (SN)

Living by herself, Mrs. Amabel is a 72-year-old African-American who suffers from diabetes, arthritis, back problems, angina, incontinence, and high blood pressure. She has had two heart attacks and a mastectomy. She has been in and out of hospitals for the past 10 years. From her monthly income of $420.40, she pays $250 for a small, poorly maintained apart-ment. In addition, she must buy diabetes test strips, insulin, and syringes to control her diabetes. Adult diapers are out of her budget, so she uses cotton pads, which she launders. She has needed a new pair of orthopedic shoes for the past five years, she says, but has not been able to purchase them. Something as simple as sugar substitute is a big expense with her income, she noted. Mrs. Amabel's doctor has been trying to get her to eat more fish, she notes, but unfortunately hamburger is cheaper.

Home and Neighborhood

The status of one's home as a limit of choice is more ambiguous because of the tendency of housing to reflect both push and pull factors. These include issues such as psychological attachment to the place, housing quality, neighborhood quality, objective affordances of the setting such as convenience and other positive qualities, and subjective affordances of the place, that is, the ability of the home and home environment to be a place at which people can truly be themselves and in charge of their own lives. The housing situations in which our informants found themselves were varied, as follows: In the suburban sample, 9 (50%) rented apartments, and 9 own row houses, condominia, or detached homes. In the city sample, 10 (30%) rented apartments, while 24 owned row houses.

Thus in terms of ownership, 33 subjects owned their own homes (9 suburban, 24 city) and 19 rented (9 suburban, 10 city). Longevity of residence is important in that the experience of key life events and the management of daily life become deeply rooted in the setting. All owners have spent an average of 34 years in their present home, while suburban renters have averaged some 6.4 years in their current apartment and city renters some 18 years. The sample, as a whole, has averaged some 26 years in their current residences.

We will comment here in greater detail on urban homeowners—the largest group of dwellers—and urban renters because they represent in many ways the poorest and most vulnerable of our informants.

Twenty-four of the frail elders we interviewed own and live in Philadelphia row houses, the small two- and three-story dwellings that make up block after block of Philadelphia's housing stock and are by far the majority of the city's residences. These elders have lived in their homes an average of 32 years (range 10–85). Their satisfaction with their homes as places to live is quite high. On a 3-point scale (3 = satisfied very much), they averaged 2.7. By and large, these homes are in the central corridor of Philadelphia, which includes South and North Philadelphia, the lower Northeast, and the river wards. These are old neighborhoods with old houses that have seen much wear and tear. In contrast to satisfaction with homes, these elders were only fairly satisfied with their neighborhoods (2.1 on a 3-point scale). However, only 8 (of 22 questioned) had definitely thought about moving, primarily for health reasons and secondarily for reasons that included safety and declining neighborhoods.

Let us stop to think about this for a moment. These figures suggest both longevity of tenure and a high degree of residential satisfaction, even though these houses are found in some of the most troubled areas of the city, a fact represented in the relatively lower neighborhood satisfaction scores. Moving may be a conscious choice for some. But it is in the adding and subtracting of possibilities that the potential option of moving runs into difficulties. People like their homes for the most part and want to stay in them and not move. Further, this may be a case where the ability to act on available choices is an option only facilitated with considerable support. The act of moving, besides being a psychologically difficult event, is physically difficult for frail elders without substantial and dedicated help even in cases in which attractive options are easily available.

The 10 respondents who rent apartments in Philadelphia stand out as having lived alone significantly longer than the remainder of our sample. (The average time living alone for city renters was 28 years; the average for all others was 14.) The average income of city apartment renters is slightly higher than that of home owners. Still, this group of city renters appears to consist of persons who have never had the means to buy a home. Most in this group have had very short marriages and spent most of their adult lives alone.

The city renters in our sample reflected a higher degree of dissatisfaction with their homes as places to live. Five said they would not want to move and five would like to. All of those who would like to move have in fact considered moving. For example, one informant preferred living with someone else, as she was especially afraid of finding herself alone in an emergency; the others are more dissatisfied with their apartments per se as places to live. None of these five has an annual income over $7,000. Two are Irish Catholic and three African-Americans. All five live in one- or two-room apartments in older buildings in Philadelphia in traditionally old working-class neighborhoods that are undergoing ethnic transformation and general decline (see below).

Five renters liked their apartments and reported no desire to move; only one has considered moving and only because of a recent rent increase. In contrast to those dissatisfied with their apartments, only one of these five has an income below $6,000 and their average income is between $8,000 and $10,000. All are white; three live in mixed-age public housing, and two in small apartment complexes in nicer neighborhoods that feature well-maintained single-family homes.

The three apartment dwellers who live in mixed-age public housing inhabit apartments that are largely identical, with a bedroom, living room, kitchen, and bath. These informants were very satisfied with their apartments. They were easily maintained and manageable given their income and health limitations. The doorways were wide enough for the wheelchair of one informant and the walker of another. There were no steps and maintenance service was available through the management office. The others who were happy with their apartments lived in nicer neighborhoods of Philadelphia in buildings that were adequately secure, clean, and maintained.

Mrs. Coleman (SN)

One of these, Mrs. Coleman, lives in Chestnut Hill, often said to be the the most "exclusive" neighborhood in Philadelphia, in an apartment set back off the street by a courtyard. The neighborhood is very quiet and is convenient to shopping and transportation. She is one of the few elders in our sample who uses public transportation on a regular basis. She and her husband lived in the same area all of their married life. Her husband's poor health kept him from working regularly and his medical bills were a financial strain on them. After their children married and left home, they moved from a rented house into an apartment to save money. Mrs. Coleman moved into her current residence 20 years ago with her husband. He passed away 2 years later and she has been in this apartment alone the 18 years since his death. She has had frequent and friendly interaction with her neighbors, especially those in her stairwell.

She said she is very satisfied with the layout of the apartment, which she feels is easy to take care of and organized to maximize comfort and privacy. Her front door opens onto a small entryway with closets. She likes her ability to speak to someone at the door without them seeing into the apartment and was also pleased that her bedroom was at the end of a hallway setting it off from the rest of the apartment. She said that at present she was "fairly satisfied" with her home but explained that until recent changes of owner and building management and subsequent rent increases, she was "very" satisfied. The rent increases have forced her to begin looking for a new apartment, but if she had her choice she would stay where she is.

Miss Hatton (SN)

Miss Hatton was the only other city apartment dweller in our sample who is satisfied with her residence. The homes in her neighborhood are large stone buildings with yards, which are uncommon in Philadelphia. She never married and lived with her parents until they passed away. She first moved into a small apartment that she refers to as a "bleeder" as it was small, dingy, and poorly maintained. She then moved into an apartment on the third floor of a building owned by a doctor. As long as the doctor owned the building, it was well kept and her rent was not increased. After 20 years there, the building changed ownership and the rent increased. She then moved out, to her current apartment, 16 years ago.

She hopes never to have to move from this place. She lives close to her several sisters here, and the apartment, on the ground floor, is comfortable, manageable, and reasonably priced. She is very happy here. It is a one-bedroom apartment with a living room and kitchen. Her collections of china and porcelain figurines are displayed around the apartment.

Unfortunately, Miss Hatton suffered a stroke a year and a half ago and it is now very difficult for her to walk or to use her hands. She also has diabetes and arthritis. She has had a railing installed along the wall of the hallway in her apartment. Two years ago she fell and was unable to reach the phone to call for help. She had to wait for help until a neighbor heard her yelling. In keeping with her desire to continue living independently, she has a cordless phone that she always keeps within reach. She microwaves prepared frozen meals since she can no longer withstand the effort of putting together a meal and is afraid of dropping a hot pan if she tries to cook for herself.

Unlike Mrs. Coleman, who can still get out on her own to run errands and does most of her housecleaning herself, Miss Hatton cannot get out. Instead she relies both on her sisters and on the son of her old boss to do her shopping and errands. A homemaker does her laundry and cleaning. With some knowledge of options and the economic means to carry them out, Miss Hatton has been able to make several adjustments to her disability that have enabled her to continue to use the space in her apartment without any extreme reduction in the quality of her life.

Both women live in apartments that are secure, well maintained, and manageable given their health limitations. Until recently both apartments were financially manageable as well. Just as Miss Hatton had to move from an apartment she was very happy with 16 years ago because of a rent increase, Mrs. Coleman is now being forced out by price.

The other group of metropolitan renters are those five who are dissatisfied with their living arrangements. All have very low incomes. All suffer from ailments that severely limit their activity. One is bed-bound. Another rarely gets out of her chair and then only with great difficulty and with the aid of a walker. The others can walk and get out when necessary but do so very infrequently, not knowing whether they will be able to or not. They all noted they feared falling while out alone.

All live in deteriorating and impoverished neighborhoods. Only one of the buildings is said to be adequately maintained by the landlord. Two of these elderly women have lived in their apartments for 11 years, during which neither apartment has been painted. All complain about their neighbors, said to be too loud, not to take adequate safety precautions with the common entrance, or to be the cause of unsanitary conditions in the building. Throughout the interviews, for example, one woman sat armed with a can of insecticide spraying cockroaches as they came near her. Roaches were crawling down the walls from the upstairs apartment and she commented that at times they even crawled into her bed.

Why don't these people just move if their living conditions are so poor? Once again, we must consider the political economy of choice as it relates to the ways people might feel about themselves. There may be a nagging or insistent awareness that moving is or should be an option. Indeed, one may argue that society organizes information to make it unavailable to some. The knowledge of choice may be in place, but it may be experienced more as a theoretical possibility than as something a person is empowered to do. And finally, the ability to act on the possible choices is not merely a mechanical absolute but is facilitated within the complete realm of human social action. Thoughts need to be changed into beliefs and these into action. Such a process is managed by others in the best of circumstances. For the frail, old, and poor, some lacking social supports, this is not the best of circumstances. And in some cases there may be other positive aspects of this home or location that compensate for the horrendous living conditions and represent a strong "pull" to stay, as for the informant who lives in an apartment near the church that is the major source of her activities and social life.

Further, moving always involves choices of sorts and is therefore not without some substantial costs. These elders do not have much in the way of compensatory resources. Many frail elders cannot handle all the aspects of moving by themselves. At the very least, they require someone to assist in locating a new apartment, to help pack, move, and unpack. It is unlikely that they will find an apartment less expensive than the one they currently occupy; for example, two of these women live in church-owned buildings with fairly low rent. Also, landlords are often content not to raise the rent knowing that if the older resident were to move out, they would have to invest money in repairing the apartment before it could be rented to a new tenant. Additionally, there is the element of fear. These people are familiar with their surroundings but they do not know what a move will bring. Many times during interviews, informants expressed the fear that they may be "jumping from the frying pan into the flame." They are often unaware of the options available to them. Many assume that they must find another apartment or go into a nursing home. They would rather remain in familiar squalor then risk the unknown. Of this group, Mrs. Kellahan (see below) is the most extreme example of one who chooses to remain in her home despite the poor condition of the home.

Neighborhood

Our informants have lived in their current homes an average of 26 years. In fact, 15 of our informants have lived in their present homes for more than 40 years, 22 for more than 30 years, and half have lived in their homes for more than 20 years. Only 11 have moved there within the past 10 years.

When asked whether they liked their neighborhood very much, a little, or not much, 54% of our study sample said very much, 27% said a little, and 19% said not much. Suburban residents liked their neighborhoods more than city residents. Informants were also asked about the convenience of their neighborhoods for shopping, getting medical attention, visiting with friends, and their satisfaction with the privacy, noise, neighbors, and condition of other houses. On a 3-point scale (1 = low satisfaction), the overall average score was 2.42, which is high considering the objective deficiencies of many of the neighborhoods our informants inhabited.

Some 21 informants (44% of enumerated informants) have considered moving while 26 have not (56%). The reasons subjects gave for considering moving included health problems (13); dissatisfactions with the neighborhood, 9 (which included safety reasons, 7; ethnic changes, 2); no longer having ties to the neighborhood, 1; preference for a nicer area, 1; preference for a more convenient area, 1; evicted by the city, 1; high degree of dissatisfaction with the home as a place to live, 11 (which included poor apartment maintenance, 3; home expenses too high, 2; dissatisfaction with the building, 4; home in disrepair, 1; small size, 1); prefer not to live alone, 1; have merely considered options, 2.

After 20 or 30 years a neighborhood is no longer the same place one initially moved into. Long-term residents tell of population turnover, deterioration of the physical conditions of the homes in the neighborhood, and changes in the available services and atmosphere. Spouses have died and children, if any, have moved away. Friends have moved away or died and ties are not always easily made with newcomers. New neighbors often have little time for or interest in a friendship with their older neighbors. And some elders may be wary of newcomers. In the city it may be that the new neighbors are of a different ethnic group and do not speak English. For example, our city sample mentioned African-Americans, Hispanics, Indians, Cambodians, Puerto Ricans, Cubans, and "League of Nations," as sources of jarring ethnic differences. Only Blacks were mentioned by whites in the suburbs as potential "problems."

The influx of new immigrants with distinctive and often misunderstood and misinterpreted cultures has led to the emigration of many of those established residents who have the resources necessary to make a move. Houses are sometimes left vacant or rented out, as we will see in the case materials presented later. Vacant houses are sometimes occupied by squatters or used by drug dealers and users or are susceptible to fire. North Philadelphia, where the majority of our city sample lives, has a high crime rate and a recognized problem with drug trafficking and use. The risk to residents is real; these are not safe neighborhoods. Some informants noted that it is common, in their neighborhoods, for young men to approach cars at stop signs to sell drugs. Drug-related shootings and violence are common.

Most of our city informants are aware of the potential for crime in their neighborhoods and take precautions. The choice of whether or not to participate in the neighborhood and utilize its resources is in part influenced by the perceived threat of victimization. The fear of crime combines with the reality of their physical limitations, more often than not, to keep even the more mobile frail elders at home. These are people who, if knocked down, cannot get up. They know that their age, their canes, their walkers, or their slow pace mark them as easy targets. They are afraid to confront noisy children because they have no recourse against vandalism or attack.

As neighborhoods change and neighbors die off or move away, it is often the case that interaction by senior adults with neighbors decreases. The difficulty of creating new social ties in later life will be discussed in the section on social network. However, it is important to note that, significantly, *some 22 out of the 48 respondents who completed a social relations profile did not include any neighbors at all in their social networks.* And, as part of their social networks, 12 informants listed only one neighbor, 8 listed two, 5 listed three, and only 1 listed five. Instead of relying on neighbors to the extent they might in more settled or well-integrated communities, these frail elders call local relatives (if any) or social workers, or in many cases let difficulties go unattended.

In addition to pervasive fear of crime and a less common distrust of neighbors, health problems and limited mobility are also major determinants in the choice of many frail elders not to utilize the resources their neighborhood may offer. With failing health, uncertainty and fear may increase. The community resources that were once adequate no longer are so. A neighborhood that was once considered very convenient, having a grocer, an employer, public transportation, and other services all within a few blocks, becomes inaccessible to many frail elders. It may no longer be easy to walk several blocks and may be impossible to carry purchases home, tiring to wait for a bus, and painful to climb up its steps.

We found the the desire for improved transportation service was a common request of frail elders we interviewed regardless of income level and neighborhood, city and suburb alike. No one in our sample lived more than four blocks from public transportation yet only 14 people (27%) actually used it and only 9 (17%) used public transportation at least once a month. Those who did use public transportation on a regular basis were not completely satisfied with it. Health problems made access and use difficult; they worried about incontinence, about falling, and about not being able to climb up or down quickly enough.

Senior citizen transportation is available in Philadelphia and its suburbs; 18 people in our sample used these services. Senior citizen centers usually provide transportation to and from the center for their clientele.

There are various organizations like Share-a-Ride, Keystone, and Para-transit, which service the elderly and handicapped by appointment, for cost. Most of these services charge no more than bus fare. Unfortunately, these transportation services are often unreliable, inflexible, inconsistent, and inconvenient. Many require scheduling a few days in advance of a trip, and in return they guarantee pick up within two hours of an appointment. Passengers must also arrange their return in advance; often this is unpredictable because of the uncertain time necessary for a doctor's visit or hospital outpatient tests. The number of stops and number of parcels may also be restricted. This system thus precludes frail elders from setting aside one day to go to the doctor, the bank, grocer, and hairdresser. Instead, they must decide which has the highest priority and hope to make that appointment on time.

Certainly, some of the difficulties related to limited mobility and re-duced participation in the neighborhood are compensated for by formal social services and the benefits of technology. Social services bring re-sources to the frail elder. Services vary in availability, reliability, and adequacy. Services available include homemakers, visiting nurses, priests, nuns, ministers, meal delivery, and phone contact programs. Although these are designed to deliver many necessary services to the elderly, the frail elders in our sample were often unaware of what was available or how to get access to them.

Neighborhood qualities do not seem to be the single determining factor in consideration of moving. Those who live in "bad" areas are choosing to retreat into their homes and put up with inconveniences in the neighbor-hood. It is expensive and risky to move. It seems that it is only when they can no longer care for their homes that they begin to consider moving. Those who like their homes will stay regardless of the neighborhood. They feel comfortable inside their familiar space. A few vignettes will describe these concerns.

Mr. John Peters (SN)

Mr. Peters lives in the Hunting Park neighborhood, which is now notorious in the Philadelphia area press as a drug and crime neighbor-hood and has been visited by numerous local, state and federal politicians at election time to announce their plans for getting tough with drugs and crime. It is a residential area, and once predominantly white working-class residents have largely been replaced by predominantly Hispanic working-class residents. The houses on his street are almost all two-story row houses and several on his block are vacant and boarded. The house next door to Mr. Peters' is vacant but not even boarded. There were never many, if any, people out on the street when the interviewer visited.

Mr. Peters differs from most of the other city residents in our sample in that he says he does not, nor did he ever, identify closely with his neighborhood. During his career he worked in the historic district of Philadelphia and he speaks nostalgically of that area.

Mr. Peters did think about moving to a nicer neighborhood. He spoke of moving to a place that would be better suited to his disabilities, where transportation was more accessible, and with no stairs. One possibility he has considered is Center City.

SN: Are there things about your neighborhood that are cause for worry?

JP: Yes.

SN: Like?

JP: Crime. Fires.

SN: I noticed that a large number of houses are boarded up on this block. Does that worry you?

JP: It does. Two years ago this house next door to me burned. The lady that lived there she died the same year as my mother. She would hide her face in shame, she was so proud and worked so hard on her home. She was an old lady, probably in her eighties. Nobody knew for sure. But her house burned two years ago. It's never been repaired. It hasn't even been boarded up. Homeless people go in and out. I think it's not only unsightly but it is dangerous. I've tried. My neighbor has tried. I've reported it to my primary social worker. But nothing gets done. Nobody knows who is responsible for it.

SN: What do you like least about living here?

JP: I would have to say the deterioration of the neighborhood. My brother, I don't think he had been in this house for years. He's invited me to his home, but he never came here. He doesn't like this street. He thinks that the most terrible thing I can do is to continue to live on this street . . . I think it is a running away. If you don't like something, get away from it. My attitude is try to improve it or at least put up with it.

Mrs. Thelma Miles (SN)

Another informant, Mrs. Miles, lives in a neighborhood with a great deal of drug traffic and drug-related violence. She noted, "It's hard to go out here because you can be standing on the corner and somebody come up and snatch your pocketbook or whatever. If you don't have nothing they might beat you up or you know. I've never had that happen to me as yet. But, there is a first time for everything."

Mrs. Miles has taken every precaution to protect herself from crime. She had a high fence installed in her backyard; she has had bars placed on all of her windows; her large German shepherd is stationed in the back; she owns a gun; a baseball bat is kept near the cellar door; she is active in the neighborhood Town Watch program; and she does not open her door to anyone after dark.

She noted, "I don't need no six-room house. And, I'm not gonna rent no rooms out to anybody. Because, unless it be an elderly person, because there's so much drugs and you don't know who's on drugs and who's not on drugs. You just have to be careful and take your chances. But, I'm scared. So, that's why why he put that security door on there. I can lock in and lock out. One of my neighbors has a key. If they don't hear from me, they come see about me. I have some good neighbors. Pretty good neighbors."

Although Mrs. Miles has a small group of neighbors that she trusts, she is aware of the danger in her neighborhood. "I feel much safer in the house. Out in the streets you don't know when you're gonna run or not. With these people out here. Like, last week, last Wednesday my dog was barking so, and I wondered what was wrong. He has a different bark when he barks for people, then he does for the dogs. I went to the back door and there were two narcotics policemen right there by my fence with their guns cocked at the house over there. They were trying to get my dog to keep quiet, so I took him in the house. They were trying to make a bust. They made their bust, I was glad they did because it's terrible around here. There is so much happening. I know you heard about the shooting in the other block. [There was a drive-by shooting at a drug house.] It's bad. You can't be too careful. So, I feel safer in my house. It they try to come in on me in here they are gonna be hurt. They are either gonna be in the hospital or the morgue because I'm not gonna play. Whatever I have, I'm not gonna let anybody in my house no way. But whatever happens, I don't open the door at night. If they don't call me on the phone and tell me they are coming they don't get in. I lock my doors. If someone tries to break in I have bars. I paid good money to get the bars and to get that high fence out there. By the time they break the windows to get the bars off you can have the police here."

SN: How long has the house next door to you been boarded up?

TM: Since before Christmas [almost a year]. They go in these empty houses and cook that stuff. And the squatters get in there. And they can set the place on fire. It's scary.

SN: What are some of the best things about living here?

TM: Nothing good now. It was a lovely neighborhood . . . Well, the neighbors are nice. The ones I bother with, I don't bother with all these people. The ones I bother with are just down this end. I know some of the others but just say hello or good-bye. Down this end of the street we look out for each other. Like, I'll be sitting at the window and I see somebody strange going on her porch. I'll call them on the phone to see if they are home. If it look like they are trying to break in I'll call the police that's all. That's the way we do.

Mrs. Miles went to Harrisburg, the state capital, with a group of senior citizens to protest crime in the neighborhood. She noted, "We worked hard for our homes. We don't want to leave."

Edna Bellman (SN)

Edna Bellman moved to the Fifth and Olney area when she was a very young child and at that time the now-urban area was "countrified." She left the area when she first married and lived in Germantown, another neighborhood, for years and in the suburbs. She returned to Olney to care for her mother and she is now living alone, bed-bound, in her family home. She reminisces about the old dirt roads, the convenience of the neighborhood in later years once it began to be built up, and the services all within walking distance. Since she no longer goes out, she feels the changes in the neighborhood are now unimportant to her. She noted, "I'm not out in the neighborhood now. But the neighborhood had gone down, as you know. That wouldn't worry me much. It's like any other neighborhood. What is safe today?"

Henry Anton (SN)

Henry Anton is 83 years old and suffers from colitis, the effects of a broken hip, and heart disease. The neighborhood he lives in is a poor, mostly residential area, consisting primarily of two-story row houses. A few in his area are boarded up but many are covered with graffiti. During the early afternoons when the interviewer visited, there was very little life visible on the streets other then young drug dealers. On several occasions, the interviewer was approached at stop signs. Once two young men came up to her as she parked and got out of her car, about a block from Mr. Anton's house. One asked what the interviewer needed, then began to list drug items he had. His colleague said, "Leave her alone, she's a lady cop. She has a tape recorder in that bag." (How did he know?)

Mr. Anton speaks openly about the problems of drug trade in the neighborhood. But he said that he does not feel threatened or endangered. He said, "I don't bother them and they don't bother me." He also feels that as long as his immediate block is not affected then the problem is at a sufficient and protective distance. Since he does not often leave his home, he has no reason to fear being victimized on the street by either drug users or drug dealers. His house provides sufficient insulation from the neighborhood crime, he feels.

Mrs. Edith Amabel

Mrs. Amabel, previously mentioned, lives right off Broad Street, the main north-south thoroughfare in Philadelphia. The entrance to her apartment is around the side of the building, not far from a church. There is a busy subway station at no great distance and a bus stop on the corner. She complains of street people stashing their belongings in the hedges behind her building, of their "coming back here and using it as a bathroom." Intruders easily go unnoticed. She worries about the addicts and street people wandering around, noting, "they have nothing better to do but watch me come in the door."

Her apartment has been broken into on several occasions. They removed the bars from the window and entered through it. In response, she now tries to leave the radio on and to change her light usage patterns. During interviews, she was always aware of any movement in the alley between her house and the church. She said, "Whenever I get one of those nervous feelings like there is someone on the side, I ask the Lord to take care of me."

Mrs. Iris Summer (SN)

Mrs. Summer lives in the Spring Garden area, a quasi-gentrifying area not far from the Philadelphia Museum of Art. She is 79, has heart disease and arthritis, suffers from shortness of breath, and has poor eyesight. Her immediate neighborhood is hard to characterize. Around the corner from her home is a lot where neighborhood men sit, smoke, and talk. In contrast, a few blocks in the other direction is a very trendy cafe catering to the young and well-heeled. Her apartment overlooks a playground. "Sometimes they go into the playground and smoke their drugs. But the neighborhood is okay. It's quiet. Nobody bothers me."

Mr. John Rose (SN)

Mr. Rose is 82 years old and suffers from severe arthritis and circulatory problems. He, too, lives in Spring Garden, and his immediate neighborhood is predominantly black. He lives across the street from an overgrown vacant lot. This frightens him. He noted, "You never know who might jump out." But his main complaints are about the other tenants in his building. The man upstairs is "a faggot and there are men coming in and out all night." There are also a few young children in the building and their playing and voices disturb him. All of these people are never as careful about locking the front door as he would like them to be. This concerns him because his door is right inside the entrance on the ground floor. Although Mr. Rose would like to move, his home is important to him as a place to sit or lie down when the pain of his arthritis hits him. For this, privacy and quiet are essential, he feels.

Fear

Neither the subjective nor objective experience of home can be considered independently of one another or of the conditions that affect choices. Mrs. Kellahan's living conditions and attitudes about her home provide us with our most extreme example. Although it is our preference throughout this book to allow the elders to speak for themselves, in this case we would like to use the interviewer's subjective and objective assessment and reaction to Mrs. Kellahan's home, along with Mrs. Kellahan's own feelings about it.

What follows is not an overreaction to urban squalor. A large portion of our metropolitan sample live in conditions that would be judged inferior by any standard for a progressive society. And Mrs. Kellahan was interviewed near the end of our research, so we had already interviewed nearly 50 elders in Philadelphia and our research team has had the experience of interviewing many hundreds of people over the years. (In addition, the authors have lived in or near Philadelphia and are quite familiar with a variety of neighborhoods and the conditions that exist in them as well as, first hand, a variety of Third World urban slums and squalor.) We are quite fortunate that Mrs. Kellahan was not excluded from our study.

Mrs. Kellahan (SN)

I was given the incorrect address and her street was not marked, so I drove around the neighborhood for quite some time looking for her apartment. There were plenty of people about, yet I would not stop and ask for directions. This was not a neighborhood that I felt safe in, and I thought better of opening my car window asking someone for directions advertising the fact that I was a stranger to the neighborhood. I had just about given up on finding the place, when I spotted a postman. I stopped, and he gave me directions.

Mrs. Kellahan lives on a small back street directly behind a bustling business area. There is a subway stop at the main intersection, and the commuter train runs above the nearby main street. Thus below the elevated railway is a street lined with a variety of businesses, such as hardware stores, clothing stores, music stores, groceries, and a check-cashing establishment. Many of these stores display their goods on the sidewalks. They cater to the local neighborhood, now primarily Hispanic. There were many people, mostly men, just "hanging out" on the side street leading to Mrs. Kellahan's back street.

Her home is adjacent to a bar, and there were two other buildings on the block, but the remaining buildings were vacant. Afraid that my car might be stolen or vandalized, I parked it in front of the shops on the main street and very self-consciously walked around the block to her apartment. When I walked up to the door, a middle-aged man sitting in a car across the street got up saying, "Wait a minute, just a minute." At first I ignored him, but then realized he was somehow connected with this building. He asked if I was there to see Mrs. Kellahan. He let me into the building and assured me he would keep the door open till I got to the first landing so that I'd be able to see. Good thing he did, because it was almost too dark to see even with the door open. The stairs were narrow, brown and dark. I focused on the wall at the head of the stairs. It was stained, peeling, and filthy. For a few steps I could not see anything at all. I was uneasy not knowing what I'd find around the bend.

On the second floor there was a closed door. I suppose it was locked, but it didn't look very secure. Once I reached the second flight of stairs I could see more—it was lit by the sunlight from the third-floor windows. These walls were even worse. Large pieces of wallpaper were falling down, stained brown.

The third floor is Mrs. Kellahan's. At the top of the steps was a large bathroom. The door was open. It did not look used, no signs of anyone living here. No towels, no shower curtain, no bottle of shampoo or soap. There were two styrofoam cups and a bottle of ginger ale in the rust-stained tub, an electric hot pot on the floor, and a roll of toilet paper on the window sill. At the end of the hallway was a door standing wide open. I called out to Mrs. Kellahan to announce myself. There was no response. I approached the room and called out again. I did not want to frighten her. Still no response. I wondered if anyone was there.

I entered the bright sunlit bedroom. There was a dresser with a few things peeking out of open drawers. A walker with a white crocheted shawl and an adult diaper draped over it stood in the middle to the room. A large armchair was strewn with a few stuffed animals and a small desk was covered with papers. There was a small cardboard chest of drawers. Other papers, a calendar among them, were scattered on the bare floor. A set of luggage was standing upright near the armchair. Beside the bed was an end table with a lamp, a clock, some papers, eyeglasses, and some Tylenol bottles. There was a large trash bag on the floor beside the bed. A small dinette chair was pulled up close to the bed and used as a table.

The bed itself was small, a bare, blue, worn mattress on a steel frame. Two mouse traps were set under the bed. A blue wool blanket was folded and crunched at the foot of this tiny bed. A comforter was haphazardly thrown across the bed. Until I glimpsed the sole of a foot under this stained comforter, I was still uncertain of her presence. Only then was I able to make out the faint outline of a tiny person in a fetal position under the comforter. (That word seems so ironic!) Her back was toward me. She was naked from the waist down, and a cloth diaper was spread on the mattress under her hips. I wanted to leave. I did not want to wake her, nor did I want to discover that I could not. I wanted to cry.

I neither left nor cried. I called her name again. She woke, she jumped. A very thin arm with long crooked fingers rose up to shield her face from whoever or whatever was intruding on her sleep. It was a pitifully defensive gesture. After a moment her huge blue eyes tried to focus on me. Her body relaxed after being startled from sleep. She greeted me still unsure of who this intruder was. I introduced myself. She asked for her glasses. Finally, she pointed one of those long fingers at me and said, "I've never seen you before."

During my visits she never moved from her half-fetal position. She lifted her head up from the bed now and then as she spoke, but she'd set it back down to rest. She twisted around to answer the wall phone right above her bed. And she'd gesture now and then with her arms, always bringing them back under the covers when she was done. She enjoyed talking. She had things she wanted to say. She was honest. She was humorous. And she laughed at her own jokes.

Mrs. Kellahan is 85 years old, a Catholic of Irish descent. She was married once, but left her husband more than 50 years ago and has no children or other family still living. She has lived in this same apartment for 38 years. She used to love this home, she said. It was pretty and well kept. She reminisces about how comfortable it was and how satisfying it was to come home to it. Now, it frightens her.

Mrs. Kellahan repeatedly spoke of fear. She is afraid of the home itself. Afraid of fires, collapse, mice, cockroaches. "I'm afraid it is going to fall down. I am afraid of the electricity. A repairman once told me the whole place is falling apart, that it needs to be rewired. And the plumber told me not to lean on the tap, that the pipes are about ready to collapse . . . I freeze in the winter and bake in the summer up here."

She is afraid of the neighbors. A man in his forties, Juan, lives on the floor below her. She is dependent on this man's whim. She only gets food when he offers to get it for her. She cannot call him. He often comes into the room unbeknownst to her, much as the interviewer did. Mrs. Kellahan explained how he sneaks up into her room in the middle of the night. She doesn't hear him coming. She said that there have been times when he comes as late as 10:30 at night. She wakes up and finds him in the room looking through her things. Once he tried to come up at two in the morning, but he tripped and fell coming up the stairs. He has taken money from her on several occasions. Although he has not physically hurt her, she worries about it. "Why would he come up in the middle of the night unless . . . What does he want to do kill me, rape me, or steal from me?" She complains of having no privacy, no safety. She cannot lock her bedroom door. Mrs. Kellahan is especially worried about the summertime when it will be too warm for her to cover herself with a blanket. Then he might come in and find her uncovered. In the winter, her covers were all that protected her from intruders.

Mrs. Kellahan fears the neighborhood. When she was still able to get up the stairs she'd often sit out on the steps. She claims to have been robbed 16 times and in several of these incidents she was knocked down. Other complaints she had about the neighborhood included the fact that the only food available was Puerto Rican, the street was too noisy, and the conversations that drifted through her windows were vulgar and insulting, and that no one would dare come visit her and even cab drivers refused to come into this area.

Mrs. Kellahan also fears change. She admits that she needs help, medical and otherwise. She has not seen a doctor in over five years. She said, "I am afraid of what they will tell me. I am afraid of what I know. I know it is serious. They will want to keep me in the hospital, I know it is serious. I need treatment for my bladder." She admits to not being able to care for herself. "What I need is a maid. I can't get out and get things for myself . . . I don't even have enough pep to get up and boil water for coffee or instant oatmeal." Mrs. Kellahan has a room that she used to use as a kitchen, but it has no refrigerator or sink. There is an old unused gas stove. So she is completely dependent on getting her food from outside. Only Juan, and a friend who visits every couple of days bring her anything. After the first visit, I always brought a lunch for us to eat during the interviews. Both times she quickly ate her share, and accepted my offer to leave mine for her to eat later. On one occasion when I brought a thermos of coffee, she did not stop raving about how good it was. She had not had hot coffee in a long while.

This place is no longer home for her. She can remember when she loved it, when she "couldn't wait to get home from work, because it was so peaceful." It was like a paradise, she felt. Now it has become a burden. "I would not mind leaving. I am scared here. The only time I relax is when

I'm asleep." (Considering her reaction when I woke her, she probably doesn't even relax then.) She continued, "Nobody with any common sense would consider this place safe. But where can I go? How can I live on $431.00 a month? No one can live on that, not comfortably. I give more than half of it to Juan for food. I pay $130.00 a month for rent. That's cheap by today's standards but not on my income.

"It used to mean everything to me. Now I don't have no home. As far as I am concerned I live in a shack. Too bad someone won't adopt me. I would be happy if someone told me they had a basement that they would fix up for me. People live in basements. I would be happy to live in a basement. Don't you want to adopt me?"

A few weeks prior to our interviewing Mrs. Kellahan, she had been brought to the attention of the local Area Agency on Aging. Someone from this agency had come to visit her and to conduct a home assessment. The gentleman spoke with her about moving. He offered to help locate a vacancy for her in a adult care boarding home. She agreed to move if they found something. Then, when a place was found, she said she didn't want to go. Again it was fear that she talked about.

The move scared her. She didn't want to move into a neighborhood she didn't know. She still feels attached to this neighborhood and the way she remembers it. She was unwilling to give up her privacy and share a room, yet she complains of her lack of privacy here. She is afraid she won't get along with her roommate. She said, "I am always afraid that I will intrude on other people if I live with them." She does not want to turn her Social Security check over to the boarding home. She said they will take her check, provide her with room, board, and care and give her $30.00 a month spending money. "That's not enough to buy a postage stamp," she noted.

She was afraid to move somewhere that she had never seen. She also was concerned that she could not move before she saw a doctor. She would not go out to a doctor looking the way she was. She'd first have to fix her hair and cut her toenails. But only a doctor could cut her toenails, so, she would just never get out at all.

Mrs. Kellahan knows that her home is not safe. She knows that the neighborhood is dangerous. She knows that she needs care. She will admit that her home is not fit for human habitation. She will admit that she is scared to death there. But it is easier for her to live with the familiar fears and discomforts than to think about facing new ones.

3

The Altered Ethos of Choice
among Frail Elders
Living Alone

The human poignancy of Mrs. Kellahan's story is very real and very near. Our immediate reactions are often: What can we do to help? Isn't somebody responsible for this? She must be mentally ill. Why doesn't she move? How can we let this happen? Doesn't she have any family? (The answer is no.) Isn't it her own fault? She should take better care of herself! All these reactions no doubt resonate to something that is in some way true about the situation.

Luckily, Mrs. Kellahan's story is unusual, although the vulnerability of frail elders and the environmental decrepitude, fear, and feelings of threat in which many live is not. On a more analytical level, her story throws into relief three very important aspects of the lives of frail elders who live alone that together represent an altered ethos of choice among these senior adults and that will be discussed in this chapter: first, the development of a culture of living alone, that is, a set of issues and concerns common to elders who live by themselves; second, inhabitation of a world writ small, that is, once access to the larger world is cut off for various reasons, the intensive development of a multifunctional world in the remaining life space; and third, the presence of vectors to the outside world in the form of social support—relatives, family, friends, neighbors, social workers, and others who act as the impaired person's representative and agent in the larger world.

Mrs. Kellahan's case highlights these issues in a radical and unfortunate way. For her, living alone entailed certain potential options and chores as well as necessities. Her world was miniaturized to the extreme, diminished as it was to one bed and one chair in one room. Her access to the outside world was limited, uncertain, and dangerous.

The Culture of Living Alone

Under the best of circumstances, many older people would choose to live alone, once their children were grown and once they were widowed. Living alone, as a life-style, incorporates selectivity and the ability to choose, especially when adequate income and health underlie the enactment of choice. For some, such a life-style may represent mastery and control, and continued competence especially when a subjective sense of these may be subjectively compromised through illness or misfortune. Older people often mention the ability to schedule one's time and activities and the difficulties engendered by potential conflicts with others as benefits of this life-style. It is important, however, to be careful to distinguish between living alone disguised as choice and living alone as really chosen. Often, the terminology of choice is the only natural language persons have to describe the situation they are in. "For lack of a better term" often relates directly to "for lack of a better situation."

In an important sense, the structural exigencies of living alone may demand or bring about a shared set of situational realities in later life, thus facilitating an adaptational *culture of living alone*, which may be defined as shared reactions to a similar set of circumstances created by living alone in later life. Such shared reactions include the need to manage one's own activities of daily living in a meaningful way; the need to construct and keep a daily schedule; the need to construct and maintain extradomiciliary support and help; the need to regulate and maintain the flow of people coming in; the need to pass the time by combining an adequate number and type of special and mundane activities; and the need to maintain an identity and sense of lifetime coherence that may have once included others as closer and more intimate. In addition, and for our subject group in particular, the issue of health maintenance is of particular importance in the context of living alone. The need to confront health problems and potential emergencies that may arise without immediately available help is of great concern. Further, there is spillover that, while not intrinsically germane to living alone, may be associated with it, for example, not having someone immediately at hand to remind the elder to take medicine, to organize medications, to put in eyedrops, or immediately to purchase over-the-counter medications, such as cough drops or aspirin, that healthy persons are able to obtain readily and without even a second thought.

Styles of adaptation to living alone may in fact be different in the extreme. What is accepted by or desirable for one person as an adequate solution to one of these issues may be rejected by another in favor of a more satisfying outcome. However, these reactions are driven by the common experiential problems of the living situation. Other living situations, of course, engender their own distinctive sets of problems or related problems which must be handled in a different framework.

The construct of choice is very evident among the reasons frail elders give for living alone. One question presented to informants during our interview was as follows:

People live alone for different reasons. Some live alone because there is no other place to live. Others live alone because they prefer being independent. How is it with you? Do you live alone (1) because there is no other place to live? (2) because you prefer being independent? (3) because you just enjoy living alone? (4) because there is no one to come live with you? Respondents were free to give other answers, but all selected some combination of the above and, in most instances, elaborated upon these themes.

The overwhelming majority of our informants (86%) prefer living alone in their own homes; that is, 86% of our sample report that they live alone *by choice.* Of these, 40% do so because they want to be "independent." Another 22% do so because they simply enjoy living alone. The remaining 24% responded that they both preferred being independent and enjoyed living alone.

It is worth pausing here and considering what these responses might in fact mean. It is important to remember that, by and large, these are people with multiple and often severe health problems and generally low incomes, who are socially marginalized, and many have few social supports (see below). Logically, one might expect these persons to express more of a sense of helplessness, victimization, neediness, or alternatively anger at the world at large for those negative parts of their situation that derive from social process. As it turns out, these feelings do not generally receive systematic expression. Rather, if anything, there is an overwhelming sense of personal responsibility for one's own fate.

The demand characteristics of the question given above were such that subjects were forced to respond to one of the categories. They did so readily and it was quite "natural" for them to do so. The terms "choice," "independence," and "enjoy living alone" all seemed to capture something important in these informants' experiences. These words were seemingly at hand for informants when forced by the question to choose an alternative explanation for living alone. In addition, they were used extensively by informants in open-ended discussions of their lives, living alone, and their living situations. Therefore, we assume that, within the naturalistic context of their language expressions, these terms did carry meaning for our informants and did serve to concretize and condense something crucial about their life experiences and something they wanted to express to others about themselves. These words therefore must be considered programmatic statements about people that are thematic and overarching in their explanatory reach. These terms exist at the nexus between personal culture and collective culture and act as a bridge that connects, makes social, shapes, expresses, and reflects personal meaning for the informants themselves and outward, to the realm of others. Our qualitative data indicate that the major reasons for wanting to be independent are: not becoming a burden to family or friends; privacy when one wants to rest to alleviate pain or exhaustion; being one's own boss; and not having to adjust to the needs of others.

Ten percent of our elders, however, expressed a "what choice do I have" attitude, stating that they had no other place to live or had no one to come live with them. The remaining 4% gave complex responses such as "I have no other place to live, but I would rather be independent anyway."

When asked whether it bothered them to live alone "very much, somewhat, or not at all," a surprising (especially given the condition of their health) 71% replied that it does not bother them at all to live alone. Nevertheless, a sizable 29% stated that it bothers them very much or somewhat to live alone. Among these are the 15% who say they live alone by choice yet it bothers them somewhat to do so. Of those expressing the feeling that they have no other alternative, two thirds evaluated living alone negatively.

There exists a feeling, for some informants, of being comfortably set in one's ways and not amenable to change in living arrangements. For some, the thought of change is overwhelming. Realizing their physical and mental limitations, they prefer the known to the unknown even in circumstances where the unknown appears to be objectively better for their survival, if not their subjective feeling of well-being.

Living alone, in and of itself, may or may not make a person feel lonely. Relative degree of loneliness was assessed in terms of a 4-point scale consisting of 10 questions. When asked whether being alone made them feel lonely, 50% said that it did often or sometimes, and 50% said that it did rarely or never.

When asked how lonely they felt when they did feel lonely, 13% said extremely lonely; 13% said very lonely; and 74% said somewhat lonely. In response to the statement, "When I'm at home I feel lonely," 17% agreed a lot; 26% agreed a little; and 10% disagreed a little. Thus, 52% of our frail elders living alone feel some loneliness when at home, while 48% disagree a lot with the above statement, suggesting that being at home alone does not necessarily make them feel lonely.

Perhaps those feeling lonely were lonely throughout their lives. However, none of the people who agreed a lot that they felt lonely at home also agreed a lot that they were always lonely people. Nevertheless, 28% of our sample felt that to some extent they were always lonely people while 72% did not feel that this was the case.

Choices Writ Small

Given the culture of living alone and its adaptational requirements, and given the often significantly reduced life space of frail elders who live alone, the domain of choice and control itself becomes reduced and enhanced. And it may often be directed to the specifics of confronting situations and needs attendant on living alone. The domain over which a person has control and can actively make choices is reduced, writ small. This section addresses this reduction.

In a seminal work concerning the geographical experiences of elders, Rowles (1978) has hypothesized that purely spatial changes in later life entail a variety of cognitive and experiential changes. That is, because older people become less mobile, they spend more time at home and may be more involved with the scene that is visible from their home. Further, some suggest that this view of the consequences of lessening spatial mobility exists in parallel with social changes and psychological changes that eventuate in greater interiority for the senior adult.

Rowles develops a hypothesis of changing spatial emphasis (1978, p. 196) that involves the relationship of geographic (activity) constriction leading to increased sensitivity to subtle environmental nuances: selected intensification of several experiential zones including the home, the surveillance zone, the immediate neighborhood, and through "geographic fantasy" selected "beyond zones," particularly those of special significance in the elder's past. Further, Rowles hypothesizes that "there are consistent accompanying changes in the older person's orientation within space and in feelings about the places of his life reflecting a selective intensification of involvement" (1978, p. 202; italics omitted).

This is consonant with our findings concerning geographical feelings and behaviors of our impaired informants. Yet, with the frail elders that we interviewed, there were other aspects to the issue of environmental constriction and the florescence of the intimate zone. Thus above, we defined environmental centralization as one of the key psychosocial processes that relates older person to place. Environmental centralization, or the restriction of much living space to the central and most accesible environmental zones, often focused on a multipurpose table or chair, is a process that operates *within* the home. It was characteristic, to some degree, of most of the persons we interviewed. In general, informants reduced their living space and condensed their habitual operating space.

We suggest that the phenomenon of the world writ small, the world of reduced life space and contextually altered choices of frail elders living alone, has several aspects: the use of texture and "the potential for intensification"; the emerging relationship between the control of mini-mized space and the maximization of choice; and the effect of neutral or "in-between" space. We will discuss each in turn.

Texture

By suggesting a significance for the use of texture, we are adapting an insight into urban dwellers of limited financial means described by Williams (1988), in her discussion of a group of African-American apart-ment renters. Williams noted "a passion for texture" that "emerges from the interplay of financial constraints and cultural traditions" (p. 84). This "includes a decided preference for depth over breadth, an interest in rich, vivid, personal, concrete, tangled detail. It involves repetition, density, mining a situation from many facets and angles." (p. 84). She notes, "Inside apartments I saw a love of texture in a desire to fill empty spaces with artifacts and objects and to manage the density of domestic life by weaving through it the sounds and colors and rhythms of television."

This particular image of the use of texture does not fit our diverse group of informants with great precision. This is because the image was developed for a specific cultural and class context (poor urban blacks); primarily for people in middle life; for people without uniformly signifi-cant health problems; and for people for whom high habitation density may be a problem to be solved. Williams's informants are not people who lived alone. And as Williams notes above, texture may act to regulate the use of especially crowded space in an apartment.

However, there are several elements of texture that do fit the situations of frail elders who live alone. When spaces are cut off and life space is diminished, life texture may be added through the multifunctionality of rooms. Thus what is seemingly chaotic to the outside observer obeys a new logic of ordering dictated by health needs and newly established perceptions of orderliness. Further, it is often the case that the richness of environmental detail or texture that is perceived by the resident is not perceived by the outside observer as such, without guidance and expla-nation from the resident.

Let us give an example. Mr. James Devlin, described in some detail above, is a 69-year-old double amputee who lives on the ground floor of a row house he owns, where he is confined to a wheelchair. Access to his home is gained by means of a ramp that snakes across the 16-foot frontage of his row home but that is pitched so steeply because of the narrowness of his property that it is extremely difficult for him to maneuver his wheelchair down the ramp. Without help, he is consistently confined to his home, although he can wheel himself to the top of the ramp's landing where he is able to watch the passing pedestrian traffic and the activities at the factory building across the street. At the top of the ramp, inside the front door is a landing and stairs that lead to the upper two floors where there are rooms Mr. Devlin rents out. His living is confined to an apartment on the ground floor. This consists of a small living room and bedroom at the front, a dining room and kitchen behind, and a back room, once a storage room that has been converted to a toilet and shower usable by a disabled person. Mr. Devlin spends most of his time in the front room, he says. There, with the aid of a transfer triangle, he is able to move himself from his wheelchair to his bed. Most things he needs for his daily life are immediately present. These include his television, his telephone, his bookcases filled with the novels he likes, and a sofa for visitors and on which he keeps the magazine to which he subscribes. The room is crowded, at hand, multiplex.

An outsider would describe Mr. Devlin's home as chaotic and his area as a slum. Mr. Devlin is aware of these designations but in fact says that his experience of his home and neighborhood is different. While there are many abandoned, boarded-up, and burnt-out domestic and industrial properties nearby, in fact, there are many that are functioning. While there are ethnic strangers, primarily Hispanic, who as a class of people are alien to Mr. Devlin, there are neighbors, boarders, and factory workers whom he does know, who are moderately friendly, and who will occasionally do things for him. Thus the neighborhood does have some sort of traditional fabric for him to utilize. And while his home does have insects, mice, and rats, needs painting, and is feared as a firetrap, it is his, a place he owns and about which he is in large part satisfied, he says. His room has a certain texture, a certain presentation of visual and aural stimuli that can be regulated for comfort (Rubinstein, 1989).

There is another important point here. To an outsider, his home is a mess; it violates canons of middle-class standards. To Mr. Devlin, it is consonant with his values and expresses, he agrees, a sense of who he is at the present time. There are some essential ethical questions in this conundrum of values. Does Mr. Devlin's uttered degree of satisfaction mean he is *really* satisfied with what are objective housing deficiencies and, from the perspective of wider community values, deplorable circumstances? This is hard to know precisely, and must be understood within the context of choice and possibility.

Further, we may say that the smaller the living space, the greater the potential for intensity of involvement with that space. In part, this is because what was formerly spatially expansive, carried out over a larger area with functions separated by space, is now spatially condensed with single spaces having multiple functions and uses.

Minimized Controlled Space and the Maximization of Choice.

For the frail elder with health problems and uncertainty when outside the home, space that is personally controlled becomes smaller. Most daily living takes place in considerably reduced space.

Such a reduced space represents a relatively stable life-world norm that develops in uncertain, changed, or contingent circumstances. Such a state may represent a degree of comfort or a sense of equilibrium or balance. Such a sense of naturalness comes about if a life-style can be developed that matches the demand characteristics of the reduced environment or if, as Kaufman put it concerning recovery from stroke, "normality, continuity and identity" (1988, p. 83) ensue.

In other words, older persons with multiple health and functioning difficulties may reduce the amount of lived space and taxing activities so that they may get to the point at which personal energies and abilities that are compromised by health difficulties are in alignment with spatial demands and activities that are indeed undertaken. Part of normalcy and equilibrium is reaching a point where, as a usual characteristic of everyday life, a new equilibrium is established and the illness or disability no longer "controls" the person. The person is now (once again) "free to choose" within the constraints of the diminished world.

Two types of situations can compromise this new equilibrium. The first is perceived continuing decline. Decline can be attributed by the person to the progressive course of the illness or alternatively to aspects of "normal aging." The second is periodic, acute, intense bouts of illness that may radically alter the new equilibrium.

For example, Mr. Devlin, discussed above, had recently curtailed even the very few trips he was able to take from his house because of the onset of severe diarrhea. He was unable, he claimed, to get a physician to visit him at home; an attempt to go to the doctor's office was canceled when he could not arrange proper transportation. He was afraid to leave the house because he needed to stay near a bathroom.

Certainly, one of the remarkable products of decreased life space is increased control in some domains of living. Control is exercised within the space that remains. And in the event of living alone, the older individual has an additional degree of control that derives from the solitary life-style. Such independence was noted in the first part of this chapter as one advantage older people who live alone often cite about their living arrangement. In the reduced circumstances, control is often represented in two domains, the temporal and the spatial. Seniors who live alone emphasize their complete freedom to do anything at all in their space without fear of restriction and to have complete freedom of schedule, "to do what I want when I want," as so many put it. The spatial component is in fact more complex, because through the presence of personally cherished objects with meanings from the past, or through the establishment of a subjective system of domestic order that an outsider would deem chaotic, the resident may choose to emphasize ties to the past and to a prior domestic order, reflecting family, spouse, children, and the like, or a new person-centered order. Some may never have had ties to a normatively constructed domestic setting and thus it is unrealistic to expect representation of this; others may develop domestic multifunctionality because it is the only sense of organization the constraints of their illnesses may allow.

It is at this point that we face another irony of the American value of independence. The frail elders living alone we interviewed were in some sense, even in those cases of greatly reduced capacities and life space, independent, masters of their own ship. Yet we are moved to raise the question of whether this type of independence represents a degree of "false consciousness." As we will see, many of these elders lacked children and supportive family and friends. They prided themselves on remaining independent. They lived in a society that greatly values independence but has seen the supportive and stable infrastructure of urban communities often disintegrate in recent decades. In a certain sense then, the avowal of independence by these elders, some of whom live in socially and environmentally degraded circumstances, ideologically serves as a way of masking the lack of nurturance and support by community, government, and society. These are hidden people who rarely go out and are often overlooked. They receive minimum federally and locally funded services; some services are of poor quality and chaotically presented. The services appear, by hook or by crook, to help the senior adults remain in their own homes.

While these elders maintain their independence, they do so in a society that cares very little for their plight, for the quality of life in urban environments, or for human nurturance. They sacrifice, but are also made to sacrifice, for their Independence. Without much voice by service recipients, government can cut corners here.

Neutral or "In-Between" Space

With environmental centralization and spatial constriction (the diminution of life space), living becomes concentrated in small areas and zones in the home environment. What then happens to the space that is no longer used?

As we have indicated, such "in-between" space may be closed off and not utilized, may be utilized for new purposes such as storage, or may continue in its old function but be rarely used. If a new sense of comfort or personal equilibrium is established through the adoption of operational norms in the reduced space, psychologically such in-between space can be effectively tuned out as by and large insignificant for daily life.

Yet this space has the potential to act both as a resource and as a difficulty. When it is a benefit that requires little attention and energy, such as its use as storage space or expandable space (a guest room, for example), such space is competence affirming. However, when it is a source of worry, requiring maintenance and attention, such neutral space may be a severe problem, since it cannot be simply sloughed off or simply adjusted to.

Vectors to the Outside World: Social Support, Social Networks, and Personal Agents

The third element of the altered ethos of choice that we discuss here is the role of social contact in the lives of the frail elders we interviewed. With the reduction of life space, energy, and possibility, reliance on those outside the home increases in importance.

Realizing that social networks need not, and most likely are not, static entities, we asked informants to identify those people most important or close to them at the present time. A bulls-eye diagram was used in order to elicit this information. Informants were asked to imagine that they were in the center of the circle, and that the three concentric circles surrounding them represented those people who are important or close to them. Thus, those in the first circle are the subjectively most important or closest people; those in the second circle are still important or close but less so than those in the first circle and more so than those in the third circle. Those in the third circle are less important or less close than those in other circles, but are worthy of mention. Circles could be "empty, full, or anywhere in between." For each person they named, informants were asked the following descriptive information: gender, relation to informant, age, years informant has known this person, and where this person lives. Also asked were how frequently in the past year they have spoken on the phone and seen each other, and how often they visited each other in the informant's home.

What then are the social networks of our frail, community-dwelling sample of elders like? Keeping in mind that most of our sample is female, we will describe the total sample because we do not have a large enough sample of males on which to comment statistically. Nevertheless, some interesting trends emerge. Forty-eight elders answered our social network question, 8 males and 40 females. The average number of people included in each person's social network inventory is 6.4, with a range of 1 to 17.

It was hypothesized that those age 75 years and older would have a smaller social network than those younger, due to attrition by death of former friends and relatives as well as limited opportunities to add new members to their social network. This does indeed appear to be the case in our small sample. The mean size of social network for our young-olds ($N = 13$) is 7.1 and for old-olds ($N = 35$) is 4.3. Such a difference is evident among both males and females. The mean size of the social network of the young-old men ($N = 4$) is 5.25, while the mean for the old-old men ($N = 4$) is only 2.25. The women, although having somewhat larger networks overall, display a similar pattern.

The mean social network of the young-old women ($N = 9$) is 7.9, decreasing to 5.8 for the old-old women ($N = 31$), who comprise the majority of our sample.

Overall, 75% of our sample placed most of the people who are of importance to them in the first circle, while 25% placed the most people in their second circle, indicating a degree of subjective distance in the majority of their key relations. For our total sample, the mean number of people included in the first circle is 3, the mean for the second circle is 2.2, and the mean for the third circle is 0.9. These are very small social networks.

All of our informants placed at least one person in the first circle, indicating that they all had minimally *someone* who was subjectively important to them. Nineteen percent placed no one in their second circle, and 54% included no one in their third circle.

What categories of people do these frail elders feel close to and depend on for physical and emotional comfort and survival? For purposes of comparison, they may be categorized as relatives, neighbors, friends who are not neighbors, or professionals.

Is there any difference in the type of people that comprise each of the circles? In other words, do some categories of people appear relatively more frequently in one circle rather than in another? Are, for example, relatives named as important more frequently than other categories of people?

As one might expect, this does appear to be the case. Some 38 of the 48 respondents on whom we have the most complete social network data

(79%) included relatives in their social networks. The mean number of relatives included in our informants' social networks was 3.4, with a range of 1 to 10. Nine people mentioned 2 relatives in their networks.

Friends who are not also neighbors were second in importance, with 31 respondents or 65% of our elders including them in their social networks. Professionals such as social workers were mentioned by only 10 (21%) of our informants as important enough to list on their social network though most of the informants received professional services. Due to the frequency of health problems, informants might, in fact, have included their doctors, but only one person did. This doctor was, however, a close relative of the elder and was mentioned as such first.

For those people who included relatives in their social network profiles, in which circle were they more likely to be included? Keeping in mind that some people included relatives in all three circles, 36 of the 38 informants who included relatives did so in the first circle, 12 informants included relatives in the second circle, and 9 people placed relatives in the third circle. Thus, although relatives were present in all three circles they were more prevalent in the first, or subjectively most significant, circle.

Thirty-one elders included friends who are not neighbors in all three circles, with 19 including them in the first circle, 19 in the second, and 9 in the third. These friends are as likely to be found in the first as in the second circle, but less likely to be found in the third circle.

Interestingly, only 52% of our sample included neighbors as subjectively important to them, a figure reflecting, we believe, the ambiguity and uncertainty of new neighbors (described above) as well as the reality that many valued neighbors from the past have died off or moved away.

Looking more closely at the category of relatives, we found that the 10 people who did not include any relatives in their social network survived their children or never had any. The majority (52%) of our sample of frail elders living alone are currently childless! Of these, many have children who have died. Ten (45%) of the 22 people in our sample who never had any children also do not feel close to or consider any relatives still living to be of importance to them.

We conclude from these figures that, among the frail elders we studied, *although relatives are comparatively important, our sample overall has relatively few of them on whom to rely.*

While 80% of our women included relatives in their social networks, only 62% of our men did so. Eighty-one percent of our sample who live in the city and 76% of our suburban residents mentioned relatives. Among those age 75 years old and over, one might expect less mention of relatives than the younger group, due to the probability of the death of peer relatives as one ages. We did find that 85% of our informants under age 75 included relatives and a slightly less 80% of informants over age 75 did so.

Briefly, let us look at some other categories of people included in the social networks of our sample of frail elders living alone. A similar percentage of males and females, 62 and 65%, respectively, include friends who are not neighbors. Nevertheless, women (58%) are more than twice as likely as men (25%) to include neighbors in their social networks. Men (38%), on the other hand, are much more likely than women (15%) to feel that professionals are important enough to be included in their networks.

Subjects living in the suburbs (76%) mention friends who are not neighbors more frequently than do city dwellers (58%). Those who live in the city (64%) are more likely to include neighbors than are those living in the suburbs (29%). Likewise, city dwellers are more likely (26%) to include professionals than are suburban residents (6%). Young-olds listed friends who are not neighbors more often (77%) than did old-olds (60%). Old-olds were somewhat more likely to include neighbors (54%) and professionals (20%) than were young-olds (46 and 15%, respectively). This may be out of necessity due to the less mobility of the old-olds.

In our analysis of informant social support, it also became clear to us that the social networks of many informants could themselves be characterized as *vulnerable*. By this we mean that *they were small in number to begin with and the key members were themselves ill, distressed, or aged and infirm.*

Loneliness

Five evaluative statements concerning loneliness dealt more directly with the social environments of our frail elders. Sixteen percent of our sample responded that they "often" had no one to talk to and 28% responded that they "sometimes" had no one. An encouraging 56% stated that this was "never" the case for them. Although 70% of our elders "rarely or never" feel "left out," 30% feel so often or sometimes. Unfortunately, 45% stated that they are "no longer close to anyone" often or sometimes, 63% of these feeling no longer close to anyone "often." Happily, 86% of our elders believe there are people they can "turn to" often (67%) or sometimes (18%). Nevertheless, 14% of our sample feel there is rarely (9%) or never (5%) anyone to whom they can turn when need be. This group may be in special need of community services help.

As part of our attempt to assess the loneliness experienced by the sample of frail elders, we also asked a question that pertains to their ability to add new members to their social network. The statement presented was, It is easy for me to make new friends. Seven percent felt that this was never easy and 17% said that it was rarely easy for them to make new friends. Thus, approximately one fourth (24%) of our frail elders feel they have difficulty making new friends. With past friends and relatives moving away or dying, and with a decreasing ability to care for self and home, the skill of making new friends could be an important survival technique.

The relationship between social network and feelings of loneliness was greater for some of our informants than for others. We therefore thought it would be useful to examine the lives of those for whom the size of their social network was most closely related to their feelings of loneliness. There were, of course, other people for whom this relationship was much less apparent. We will first examine the case of an informant who demonstrated the closest relationship between size of social network and our loneliness assessment scale.

Emily Quinn (JCK)

Emily Quinn illustrates a clear relationship of feelings of loneliness to social network configuration. She is a 69-year-old, Irish Catholic woman with 10 years of formal education and an annual income of only $4,596. She suffers from circulation difficulties, from the effects of a past stroke, from poor vision, from thyroid problems, and from difficulty in using her left hand. She has lived in her one-bedroom apartment in a middle-class suburb for the past two years. She has lived there alone for the past five months since the death of her live-in "boyfriend" of 17 years. This is the first time in her life that she has ever lived alone.

When I arrived for my first interview with Miss Quinn, I saw her standing just inside the open door, leaning on her walker. She is a small woman with wispy, shoulder-length white hair and sparkling light-brown eyes. Alongside the entrance to the hallway was a worn leather chair, which she later told me had been accidentally set afire by her boyfriend while smoking. In fact, he had a habit of doing such things. He fell asleep while smoking in bed at their previous apartment, causing a fire and getting them evicted.

Two end tables were on either side of her bed, which was in the living room. One had a lamp under it. She explained that she had bumped into this lamp recently and that it had fallen on her so she moved it under the table. Against the wall of the living room was a vinyl couch with a suitcase on it. Since there was no other obvious place to sit, we sat at the kitchen table.

In order to situate Miss Quinn in her present state of aloneness, it is important to explain that she lived from age 21 to 52, some 31 years of her adult life, in a setting that afforded few opportunities to make her own choices in life. She was committed by her parents to a public mental institution in spite of the discovery, years later, that she was not actually mentally ill. Thus, she knows relatively little firsthand about living independently.

Her account (verified by her social worker) of the circumstances leading to her present state of living alone in an apartment began in a neighboring state. Due to recurrent headaches and dizziness, she had exploratory brain surgery when she was 20 years old. Soon thereafter she had a stroke. The left side of her body was particularly affected. She also began radium treatments. According to Miss Quinn, the treatments helped her, but nevertheless she was admitted to a state mental institution.

In recounting her story, her speech is slurred due to a recent stroke, and she speaks loudly. Her stories at times seem jumbled or disjointed. She spoke of physical and sexual abuse she had suffered as a youth and of her father having her committed to a mental institution. She complained that her father did not tell her about her mother's death for 20 years.

During the course of our second interview, Miss Quinn described in more detail the events leading to her institutionalization: Her mother told her that she should dress up because a friend of hers wanted to take her downtown. In reality, staff from the mental institution came to pick her up at her house. Her mother told her that they wanted to interview her. Miss Quinn said that the woman doctor who interviewed her believed her story but that nonetheless she was committed. A woman doctor finally convinced her after many years in the institution to move to another ward that had more freedoms and less sick inmates.

Finally, after 31 years she was released. The head of the institution where she was living became her legal guardian. When she was released, Miss Quinn wrote a letter to her only sister asking if she could help her find housing, but the sister wrote back to her that she could be of no help. This sister, whom Miss Quinn did not include in her social network profile, sent her a $60 check for Christmas this year. Miss Quinn complained that she would have rather had a present that her sister had picked out especially for her, the way that she herself does for people she cares about. She would like to deposit this check but does not know how she can get to her bank to do so now that the central person in her social network, her deceased boyfriend's son, has moved with his family to a

New England state. In order to understand how Bryan, her boyfriend, and his son became so important to Miss Quinn, we return to the period after she left the state hospital and was living with two girlfriends from there in independent housing while working in a sheltered workshop. She met Bryan at a party given by one of her roommates. Described as very handsome, he pursued her, convincing her to date him. When her roommates moved elsewhere, Bryan got permission to move in with her. At first, the only thing she told me about Bryan was that he had worked on Wall Street. She later volunteered that he was manic-depressive and had an engineering degree. Bryan's wife had divorced him after she retired from work because she wanted to travel, Miss Quinn noted.

Bryan's family became her family. When Bryan's son moved his family to a Philadelphia suburb as part of a job transfer, Bryan refused to move there with him unless Miss Quinn could also come. The son obtained a nice apartment for his father and Miss Quinn not far from where he and his family moved. When Bryan caused a fire in that apartment, his son found them their present apartment. Not long after, Bryan's son was transferred back to New England. Unfortunately, Bryan soon died suddenly.

Bryan's second son, who lives in another nearby state, drove Miss Quinn to Bryan's funeral in New England. This was the only time she has stayed overnight away from home this year. In fact, she has not been outside a four-block radius from her home since she moved here, with one exception. For the past four months, she has been waiting for Bryan's son to find her a place in public housing in New England near where he now lives. He has assured her that he is doing his best to get her in (her social worker verified this). Her rent is paid up until next month, but the apartment owner is threatening to evict her then. Until recently, Bryan's son had visited Miss Quinn monthly and taken her to the bank and to the doctors when he did. She said that he also used to call her each morning from work.

Last week, he told her that he and his family were going on a vacation. When she called his home, a message said that the phone had been temporarily disconnected. She is concerned about this and is afraid that Bryan's son is withdrawing his help from her. She wishes that she could live with him and his family, the only people listed in her social network, but knows that this is not a real possibility. She rationalizes this by saying that there are probably too many steps in his house for her to be able to climb.

Although she has thought about living with Bryan's son and his family, Miss Quinn also said that she would rather live alone because then she could do what she wanted without a lot of disagreements like when Bryan was alive. She added that she enjoyed living alone and that she rarely felt lonely. Nevertheless, she stated that she often had no one to talk to now that she can no longer walk to the nearby shops. She bumped her head last month when trying to find her way to her bathroom and cannot walk unaided at present, gets dizzy, and has ringing in her head. She now uses a walker.

She says, too, that there are never people she can turn to and that sometimes she feels left out. She gave as an example the day she went to the senior center and did not know anyone there; she really felt like an outsider, she said. She does not really like living where she is, she adds, because she is too far away from Bryan's family and other people she knows. She noted that she is beginning to regret having ever moved here with Bryan because she feels so alone. She views her apartment as "just a place" and uses the adjective "uninteresting" to describe it. It would not bother her at all to move. She would rather live in a city where there is a lot of activity outside her door.

As I was leaving after our final interview, the man who delivers her meals on wheels arrived with a holly plant from a local women's club. She asked me to put it on the windowsill for her; then she smiled and thanked him. As he was leaving, he asked whether she would be wanting a meal on Christmas Day. Miss Quinn looked down at her hands and quietly said yes.

Anne Daley (JCK)

A very different picture is seen in the composition of the social network and feelings of loneliness experienced by Anne Daley, an informant who ranked nearly highest in the size of her social network and was among the least lonely informants. Like Miss Quinn, Mrs. Daley is also Irish Catholic. Unlike her, she has been married and widowed twice. Her health is better and her mobility much greater even though at age 77 she is 8 years older than Miss Quinn. She is one of the few in our sample who still drives her own car. However, her good health is episodic. She has suffered in the past few years from recurrent bouts of bronchitis and was recently hospitalized for a week with severe pneumonia. Her main health problems (which are under control at present) include high blood pressure, angina, which she has had for the past six years, and an abdominal abscess, like the one from which her father died. Also unlike Miss Quinn, Mrs. Daley is a high school graduate with two years of "finishing" school, a home that she owns and in which she has lived for the past 40 years, and an annual income of approximately $9,000. She has worked, mainly in secretarial positions, by choice at first and by necessity later in life. She has lived in the same area, a suburb of Philadelphia, all of her life.

There were also very great differences in the childhoods experienced by the two women. While Miss Quinn had only one sister with whom she has never been close, Anne grew up in a large family, with three sisters and two brothers, of whom three still survive.

We speak of these two informants in contrast to illustrate the point that very different life circumstances can lead to the situation of living alone as a frail elder. Of interest here is that these women reflect a relationship between social network size and quality and the situational experience of loneliness. Mrs. Daley, however, presents a case of someone who, by circumstance as well as by her own initiative, is coping well with feelings of loneliness.

Mrs. Daley described her childhood as liberating and protected. She said, "We grew up, there were six of us. We had fun. We had plenty of room, plenty of space to run outside. We had a maid. And a laundress came two days a week, which I just took for granted. My parents didn't want me to work, but I wanted to work. When I got up in the morning, the maid prepared me breakfast. But if I was late, she would meet me at the foot of the steps with a glass of juice, and I would gulp it down and run for the train. I would love that kind of attention today. I think it would be perfect."

The first job she had was in a large department store. She and a friend decided it would be fun to work there. The two mothers got together and decided that they might as well let their daughters get this out of their systems. Her mother knew the man that was in charge of "the whole first floor," and wrote a note introducing the girls, but did not really believe they would get a job since they had no previous work experience. However, they were hired. She worked at her job for a few years. Then she worked at other jobs, including at an insurance company, a school for exceptional children, and a county prison. She said that every place she worked she learned new things.

She retired at age 65 after working part-time in retail sales in a local department store. She noted, "It was interesting. My two sisters said it was a good thing that I was the one who got left without anything to fall back on, because they would never have been able to go out and get a job." She talks about being in Christmas pageants at the retail store in Philadelphia where she worked. She was also in their chorus when it sang at a park with the Philadelphia Orchestra. She concluded, "It was the biggest thrill. So I got an awful lot out of what I did." As we can see, during the first portion of her life, Anne made choices to work and to learn new skills even though there was no necessity to do so. These choices would serve her well later in life when problems arose.

Mrs. Daley labeled part of her life, "Trouble After I Got Married." She sums this period up by saying, "There were some good times, but it was pretty difficult with the sickness." Her first husband got sick with a stomach ulcer six months after they got married and was sick for the rest of their 19-year marriage. He died of a heart attack in 1965. Anne describes him as a "perfectionist" who she met through friends. He was born and lived in Ireland until he was 21 years old. She noted, "He was very obstinate. You did things his way when he wanted or if he wanted or you didn't do anything. It was a very difficult time. And I also learned to just be quiet. When you argued, it was just more difficult so you couldn't. That was the most difficult part. The second time around after being on my own for four years, and enjoying being on my own, well my second husband, up until he got sick, was just wonderful. He couldn't do enough. He would come home with a present. I would say, 'What's that for?' and he would say, 'Just because I love you, no reason.' If we were invited out to dinner, I would say, 'I'll let you know,' and he would say, 'Sure. If you want to go it's all right with me.' Now with the first one you couldn't. He'd say, 'So and so? No, we're not going!' So I finally just made excuses, excuses, excuses. The second marriage was so different but it only lasted two and a half years before he got sick."

Her second husband had a massive stroke then, and she took care of him at home for almost six years before he died. He was 59 years old when he had his stroke and could not go back to work, so she got an office job at a local firm.

Mrs. Daley describes getting up at 5:00 A.M. and taking care of her husband before leaving for work. She would go to work, then come home to fix his lunch, then go back to work. It took her 20 minutes to drive home, 20 minutes to fix his lunch, and 20 minutes to drive back to work. She got home at 4:00 to cook his dinner. He was diabetic and had been on insulin for years. At first he managed to get around with his walker and could dress himself. The year before he died he had his leg amputated and learned to use an artificial limb. He died of a massive heart attack on Mother's Day.

She recounts the story of how her husband told her that her mother had called her to tell her that her sister's husband had just died that day. Mrs. Daley then went into the kitchen to get some lunch, and her husband came in shortly thereafter. He had put on his artificial leg and used his walker to go into the kitchen where she was. She asked him if he had changed his mind about wanting something to eat. As she looked at him, his eyes were bulging and he was gasping for breath. One hour after hearing of her sister's husband's death, her own husband died! This was 13 years ago.

Mrs. Daley has lived alone since then. She gets along well with her second husband's family, describing how her stepson and his wife, whom she includes in the first circle of her social network, call her to see how she is doing (about four times a year) and how they still visit one another (twice a year). Mrs. Daley sums up her feelings about her husband's family by saying, "I was really fortunate. I really got another whole new family."

At present Mrs. Daley enjoys the independence she has, she says, by living alone and no longer needing to care for someone who is sick. She is not kidding when she says that she would not marry her present boyfriend, whom she jokingly describes as an old man of 84, nor indeed any other man, for fear that she would have to go through the caretaking again. She remains active and still drives and when she can no longer drive her own car, a major adjustment will need to be made in her social network, which is quite dispersed. As with many of our suburban, as well as city, informants, the senior center will become an even more important source of social interaction.

There is one other relationship between her life events and her social network and feelings of loneliness that must be mentioned. Included first in her social network are her daughter-in-law, her 8-year-old grandson, and her 5-year-old granddaughter. Her only child, a son, would have been first on her list, but he died in an automobile accident a year ago. He was 39 and living with his wife and children in the Midwest when he was killed. After his death, his family moved back to Pennsylvania. Mrs. Daley visits them about six times a year at their home or at hers, and they speak on the phone weekly.

Mrs. Daley's personal strengths and her friends helped her through this tragedy. When asked to identify what she felt to be her personal strengths, she said, "I think one thing that helped me is that I don't let myself dwell on the hard times. For a while there, I just took each day as it came and got through it. I think that the roughest time that I ever got through in my life really was when my son was killed. And I got through that because my stepson and his wife took me to their home right after the funeral and kept me down there. I was sick. I had broken my ankle the first of January, and I had the flu the middle of the month, and I got word that he was killed the 30th. So I was on crutches, and they took me right back to their home, and I was there for two weeks. Then I flew from there to visit my sisters [who live near each other in another southern state with their families], and I was there for another two or three weeks. So actually it got me over the worst part."

She thinks that her ability to adjust to things has helped her. Her philosophy, she says, is "Anything you can't do anything about, you might just as well adjust. If you can do something about it, go ahead and do it. My older sister always said she never worried in her life because by worrying you use a lot of energy and nine times out of ten what you worry about never happens. So you've lost all that energy for no good. I

learned a long time ago after two sick husbands I think I got worried out
. . . Right now, really, I enjoy my life. I'm not lonesome being by myself. I
enjoy what I do. I enjoy being able to do what I please. I enjoy not having
to worry about taking care of people. It sounds awful to say that, but I
really do. I enjoy it now. I love my life the way it is."

There were some of our frail informants for whom the relationship
between social network and loneliness was the opposite of what one
might have expected. Two of the three individuals who were much
lonelier than their social networks would have predicted stated that they
"always" had been lonely people. The other person has many personal
worries about her family and her health. The four elders who professed
very little loneliness (in spite of having but two or three people in their
social networks) appear to be using the mechanism of denial, some more
successfully than others. One of these, 85 years old, has never married
and has no children. He judges his eyesight to be "good or adequate,"
although he is legally blind. Another is an 84-year-old woman with four
children who only has contact with her youngest son. She included only
this son and his wife and daughter in her network inventory. She repeatedly stressed her independence and how she does not need anyone. She
has had to be very self-sufficient in her life. Her first husband did not
provide financial support for her and her children, and her second husband got cancer shortly after they married. She has toughed things out.

Helen Burnhardt (JCK)

The other woman whose social network is not indicative of her feelings
of loneliness is an 82-year-old widow of 15 years who was born and grew
up in Germany. Although Mrs. Burnhardt goes daily to a nearby senior
center, she did not include any of the people who also attend this center in
her network inventory. Only two people were deemed important enough
to be listed in her network: her son, her only child, who takes her out to
dinner once a week, and a friend she has known for 14 years, whom she
now sees only twice a year, but with whom she speaks on the phone two
or three times a month.

After the death of her husband, she sold her suburban home and lived
for a short time with her son and his wife, but there seem to have been
some difficulties that she did not discuss. Mrs. Burnhardt very much tries
to present a cultured, positive image of herself and in so doing may keep
others from getting close to her for fear that she may not think that they
are good enough to associate with her. Although she does not profess to
be very lonely, she does appear to be searching for someone with similar

interests, experience, and education who would appreciate and understand the same things that she does. Since the death of her husband, she
has not found that person. Any of her own relatives who are still living
reside in Germany. Her contact with them and others is now represented
through the beautiful objects she has in her apartment as remembrances
of her family and another way of life.

Charles Emory (JCK)

One other informant's attitude to living alone as a frail elder will be
discussed next in order to understand better the complex relationship
between social network and feelings of loneliness. Like Mrs. Burnhardt,
Charles Emory also attends a suburban senior center, lives in a nearby
suburb, and likewise professes relatively little loneliness while also listing
only two people in his social network profile. Similarly, he stated that it
does not bother him at all to live alone and that he does so out of choice
because he prefers to be independent and simply enjoys living alone. In
fact, Charles Emory commented that he liked "being alone without being
lonely."

Mr. Emory was a lieutenant in the army during World War II. He
received a medical discharge after 14 years of army service because of
blindness in one eye. At present, he has cataracts in both eyes that render
his eyesight extremely limited. However, he does not admit to this and
describes his eyesight as being "fair" although he described his vision as
"hazy" (his terms). When asked whether he thought that his illness or
frailty was "controlling his life," he replied negatively but with the
exception that he needed a cataract operation, noting, "For example, I see
two of you."

Mr. Emory is a man of words and has a good sense of humor. In
describing his cataracts, he said, "I got two cataracts, one in each eye, and
I gotta have 'em taken off, and everything seems dim. But I'll live until I
die." He smiled, and we both laughed.

Several instances during our interviews led to the conclusion that Mr.
Emory tends to deny things, or perhaps to adjust to and accept things,
such as his failing eyesight or loneliness, that he does not want to face.
During one of our visits, he asked help in finding a suit that was in his
bedroom closet. Several suits were brought out before he decided which
was the one he was searching for by putting his eyes very, very close to
the material and feeling it. He also has poor eye-hand coordination when
reaching for an object, for example, when trying to put the ashes from his
cigarette into the ashtray, which sits on the couch next to his chair.

Having lived in his home some 43 years, Mr. Emory also knows his way around it very well. Nevertheless, he did get disoriented during one interview when he went into the bathroom when he meant to go into his bedroom. Both rooms are on the first floor but at opposite sides of his house. He has adapted to his poor eyesight by keeping things where he knows he can find them. For example, he places the clothes that he will be wearing on one chair in the living room and his laundry to be picked up by a service on another chair there.

His acceptance of being alone is illustrated by his response to a question about having visitors. In this regard, Mr. Emory mentioned the second person in his social network inventory, a niece who is married and lives in Philadelphia. He said, "Well my niece, the girl I raised from that high, comes up and I sometimes go in there to visit them. But they come get me and bring me in and I stay overnight or maybe they bring me back home." When, however, asked the last time he stayed overnight at her house, Charles replied, "I guess it was ten years ago."

His home is very much related to his feelings of contentment: He has less loneliness than one might expect. His home complements and is an extension of his life. In general, Mr. Emory seems to enjoy reminiscing about the good old days and his satisfaction with having lived a full life. He is proud that he was married to the same woman for 41 years and is happy with the time they had together, especially those years they shared in his present home. Although his home is a small, one-story wooden structure and greatly in need of repair and cleaning, in his eyes it is both beautiful and a comfort to him. It has an enclosed entrance porch that looked like it had not been in use for a long time but could once have been an enjoyable place to sit and view the activities of the neighborhood. There is a lawn in front of the house but this, too, is the worse for wear. The side entrance has several cement steps leading up to the kitchen and is now the usual entrance and exit point. The kitchen is small, but large enough to have space for a kitchen table and chairs along one wall. To the left of the kitchen is the door to the cellar, and to the left of that is the bathroom.

There is an entranceway from the kitchen into a small living room. From the living room there is a door to the enclosed porch and opposite this door is a door to the attic, which was used as an extra bedroom for visitors. Across from the living room is the bedroom with the double bed Mr. Emory shared with his wife. He jokes that he has to change his sheets less frequently now that he has no woman to share his bed.

When asked about his home, he said, "I love it. There's no place like home." He is proud that he owns his own home and agreed with the statement, "Owning one's own home gives one a higher status in the eyes of others." Mr. Emory especially likes the memories of his wife that his home holds for him. They had nicknames that they affectionately used for each other. He pointed to a picture of his wife and himself that is hanging on the living room wall across from where he always sits and noted, "As you can see, she was quite attractive." One would definitely agree that the young, black couple dressed in their Sunday best, were a handsome pair.

Mr. Emory emphasized that unlike the youth of today, he would never live with a woman to whom he was not married. He is a very religious person who finds comfort in his belief in God. In fact, he credited personal wisdom and a belief in God as the main factors that helped him get through difficult times. When asked whether there was anyone in whom he now confided, he replied, "Yes, God." There is a large picture of Jesus that hangs on his living room wall next to the one of his wife and him.

He refers to his home as being a part of him and says, "To have something of your own. It means a lot to me." The more I got to know him, the more I agreed with him that he and his home were well-suited to each other and that it still continued to meet his needs. One of the things about which he is particularly proud is the fact that his home is the only one on his block with a garage. The detached garage is a one-car wooden structure in need of repair with a dirt entranceway. Mr. Emory used to own a Ford Galaxy, but he sold it when he could no longer drive. He is content with the van from the senior center that takes him there daily during the week.

There are train tracks adjacent to his back yard. Mr. Emory checks his watch, which he can no longer see well, if at all, by the sound of passing trains. Thus a noise that some might find annoying is a comfort to him and in addition makes him more a part of a life in which he can no longer participate physically the way he once did.

Mr. Emory's feelings about his home can best be summed up in his own words. Coming home, "It gives me something to look forward to." He is satisfied with what might seem to others to be very little materially. He does not think of himself as old because he can still do "a little bit of everything I used to do" or at least everything he still wants to do. In general, he is satisfied with the life he has had, and his philosophy is that others should be also. He said that one should strive for the things that one can obtain, and then be satisfied with what you have or with what you have accomplished. He seems to have done just that. And although his social network is very limited by objective standards, he does not feel as alone or lonely as this might imply. It should be pointed out that he does get to socialize with others during his almost daily visits to a senior center. He is one of the four men that attend this center and he appears to enjoy flirting with the women there. He stated that this was acceptable because they knew that he was just kidding with them. He also said that he did all he wanted to do in his younger days so he has no regrets now.

He tells the story of his favorite cat who, when he got too old, just meowed good-bye to him one day and went off alone to die.

We can see in some cases how independence is seen in part as a justification for loneliness or alienation of various sorts. Even in cases of those informants who are active and involved, relations are often contingent on the continued ability to negotiate them. With frailty, the ethos of choice is altered so that what remains, after the diminution of life space, appears choice-rich. Indeed, at least some individuals with soured relations see this state as evidence of independence. What is absent in all these cases, even among those informants with an active and supportive family, is a feeling of community context. The role of the individual in community life has certainly been hampered by policies that do not afford communities precedence and emphasize individual behavior and achievement at the expense of community values and identity.

II

SOCIALIZATION FOR CHOICE MAKING
AMONG FRAIL ELDERS

4

The World at Home

While socialization is generally thought of as a process affecting infants and children developmentally, in fact, socialization is a lifelong enterprise. Here, we acknowledge that choice making in old age is a process for which each individual has been socialized throughout the lifetime. That is, consciousness of choice, knowledge of choice, and the ability to act on available choices have all been finely developed and situated within the context of life experiences, cohort beliefs and expectations, and the changing nature of the social world.

Further, for frail elders who live alone, the dynamics of choice making, affected certainly by these and other social processes, are also shaped by the juxtaposition of residence and biography. Having lived so long in one place, having experienced bodily changes in that place, having experienced many key life events in that place, the home as an experiential setting is finely tuned to many levels of personal need. It is the residue of choices long made, or events long decided, evidence of the road taken.

While some of the informants were impoverished and impaired, many do speak of moving to their current home as an event of positive choosing. The neighborhoods were generally nicer when they came, the body healthier, the community friendlier. Feelings of imprisonment, the notion Well, what choice do I have? existed in but a few cases. For these individuals, wretched circumstances are transformed through some culturally reinforced social and psychological process, into "making do," and this into agentive individualism.

In this chapter, we begin to shift our focus from situational constraints and topical understandings to a biographical approach. Here, we examine additional aspects of the world as experienced at home, a theme taken up in previous chapters, which will continue throughout. We also lay the groundwork for a more biographical approach, a perspective elaborated in greater detail in the next two chapters. In so doing, we consider a triad of interconnecting subjects: the home, the body, and biography. The home is both a physical and a sociopsychological entity, the body a physical entity that may be in tune with surroundings, and through its health

79

history with personal biography. Biography is the point of reference for all individuals, and so the prospect of making choices can only be understood in the biographic matrix that surrounds them.

Home as a Place

While in part one is able to think of human life in a residence as a merely mechanical aspect of living or of a home as just a place, in fact, a home is more than simply shelter. Indeed, scholarly studies and widely shared personal experience have shown that homes have many functions, primarily expressive and developmental. The literature in this area is vast and it cannot be systematically reviewed here. Nevertheless, a brief act of introspection will show how much we all rely on the home for things other than shelter. Homes are places where families grow and develop; they are safe havens; they are representations of feelings, either real or desired; they are investments; they are embodiments of both our individuality and our sense of community; their messages, like a code, can be deciphered and read by others.

With age, it is clear that the relationship between aging persons and their home becomes increasingly important and intimate, because of changes in the body and in social network, and because of the affiliation of place (the home) and personal experience (biography). What has happened in life is increasingly likely to have happened in this place.

It is certainly the case that management of the personal environment is important at all ages. Our ability to shut the door, regulate who comes in, have say-so, regulate hours of sleep and wakefulness, and our annoyance and outrage when these are not respected are paramount here. We seem to be well-versed in the skills of the social house and are educated to these often unconsciously at various points in our lives: an unconscious aspect of our cultural competence. Management of the home environment is related to aspects of life such as control, independence, privacy, and expression. Outwardly, homes and their appearance negotiate the often thorny conflict between individual values and community standards and expressions.

The personal environment takes on increased importance for those who are old and frail. For example, a bump or fold in a carpet or an unevenness on a stair are things that most people who are young and healthy rarely give thought to. For frail elders, however, these may be impediments on such a scale that they need to be avoided or handled specially, and given to a special part of the consciousness that directs daily praxis.

Loss of control in general becomes more certain in later life. Changes are abundant. These include biological and cognitive changes, deaths of friends and peers, retirement, a sometimes shrinking social network, the increased possibility of isolation, and the omnipresent health issues. Triggered is a fear of the loss of autonomy for many. Consider, for example, what is entailed when one can no longer drive after one has done so all one's adult life! That sense of independence, the ability to get somewhere without having to rely on others, is gone. This is a dramatic and often painful change. For the frail elders we interviewed, their current somewhat diminished status is often subjectively juxtaposed against the possibility or threat of a nursing home. Nursing homes, while not scorned individually, are among the most consistently feared and loathed institutions in the United States. People dislike them, not necessarily because the care is bad and the staff uncaring (although they may be), but more for what they represent: the diminution of the social self. And none are more sensitive to this than those whose lives may be imminently affected by institutionalization and by the losses such institutions define.

As we and others have noted, control is spatially mediated by the constriction of space. Centralization—the conduct of the events of everyday life in limited and circumscribed space—is not merely spatial, but may affect the way one views life as well. Elsewhere, one of us (Rubinstein, 1989) has discussed the possibility that with environmental centralization comes related centralization of personal themes, the psychocultural cognitive constructs that elders and others use to guide their representations of who they are. Such themes may be thought of as key aspects of personal identity. They may be found in statements such as "I am the kind of person who . . ." as well as in other venues (Rubinstein, 1990). An empirical question for research is the relationship between spatial centralization and changes in the social self. The persons whom we interviewed for this research by and large experienced a diminished spatial life and environmental centralization. This general pattern was also reflected in their social supports.

As we have noted, there were several informants who had adequate or more than adequate social support from their in-place network of family, neighbors, and friends. But, for the most part, our frail subjects were individuals with very small social networks, which could be counted on for informal help only irregularly or under special circumstances. Several had social networks that were themselves severely truncated or vulnerable. This, too, represents a reduction of social network efficacy that is consonant with the spatial reduction in old-age frailty.

The flip side to this reduction in space is an increase in control over the space that is remaining in use. Within this reduced space, elders are able to assert their independence and make their own decisions, even though

the space is not much. Thus the personal environment becomes a significant source of autonomy, satisfaction, and pride; it is symbolic of being a
person and of personhood.

With spatial changes the home or personal environment may become
an expression of self. This occurs in several ways. The expression of self
through decor and possession are topics that have been more extensively
discussed in literature on the psychology of home. The home, too, acts
within the context of a domain of behavior that may be labeled rituals of
the self such that those important elements of decor that are portrayed
help organize memories and personal history (biography). As has been
noted elsewhere, walls of personal photographs, scrapbooks, collections,
furniture, and all the myriad of objects and objectifications embodied in
the home may at times serve to direct and stiffen consciousness of self and
act in a sense ritually to reinforce or remind the person of who he or she
was and still is, lest the self be forgotten or misplaced with the difficulties
of everyday life. It is a self that is embodied in the home. And this appears
to be especially the case for those who live alone, since they are the last
representative of the several people who may have lived there and, as it
were, the guardians of lives gone by whose stories are by now inextrica-
bly interwoven with their own.

Another important aspect of the home for frail elders is the basic ability
to command a territory. That this is a place of one's own, over which a
person has say-so, is important as both a marker and an enabler of
personhood. Lack of such command is one element that is most feared by
our informants in the threat of institutionalization. Privacy, to do what
you want when you want, a place to be alone with your memories, or a
place to be alone with your pain—were all mentioned to us by informants
as benefits of their relationship with their territories.

Part of this, too, is the realm of choice making and decision-making. To
do what you want when you want embodies the individualistic absolut-
ism of the control of decisions and choices. In many respects, our informants lacked real choices. They were tied into their homes by any
number of structural and psychological impediments. Where could they
go? How would they physically go about looking for a new place? How
could they afford it? Who would help them move? Or, how could they
afford home improvements if they were to stay in the current place? And
who would ensure the quality and solvency of the vastly deteriorating
neighborhoods? Any consideration of choice realistically must take these
questions into consideration. These were on the minds of many of the
people we interviewed. Yet because the onus of action is on the individual
and because real housing choices appear out of reach and may exist out of
consciousness, elders felt the domain of choice and decision-making to be
within their homes. Having made the choice to move into a current

residence years ago, and having stuck with it, environments were still perceived as "choiceful" and choice-rich (both absolutely and in contrast to poor-quality alternatives). And with the intensification of life with spatial concentration, this was more so in many cases.

Home was a source of satisfaction for many. We have mentioned the role of personal possessions and objects in the ritual culture of selfhood, their ability to remind people of their social and personal identity from time to time, when need be. These are more than just shrines to the past, since their efficacy is often in the present, in that they help to bring the past into the present when the past may have been forgotten or overwhelmed and it is useful now to remember it. In addition, satisfaction could be drawn from cyclic involvement in the social rituals of community life: housekeeping routines and holiday decorating, for example, that aid a subjective sense of community connection. By and large, these frail elders limited their holiday decorating and carried out housekeeping routines as best they were able.

To others, the home retains its role as an anchorage to the community. Despite a marginal existence, despite a decrepit or untrustworthy neighborhood, there is a connection to the world out there, even though it might be a remembered one. And even in these circumstances, there is always some opportunity for good neighborliness, for helping and being helped, watching out for others and being watched over.

Until it becomes a problem, the home itself can facilitate overcoming problems even when the place is awkward or difficult for the inhabitant. It helps overcome problems of living by providing the means to circumvent health-based problems themselves and by providing existential brackets to solve problems of being (see below). Given decrements, the diminution of life space and social resources, the home aids in the preservation of identity and continuity.

Yet, too, it is important to note that the house itself can become a burden, as skills and abilities diminish radically. As a burden, the home demonstrates that the control exercised over one's space is not unlimited, even with restriction and circumscription. Having too large a space; the requirements of maintenance; lack of caretaking energy; the financial strain of home upkeep; environmental barriers within the home; stairs; safety problems of all sorts; changing neighborhoods; the presence of strangers, uncertainty, and fear; crime; changing neighborhood resources; and the real presence of danger are all part of a long list of objective deficiencies that may vex these elders.

And, finally, there is the issue of owning versus renting. Clearly, owning a home presents a different set of considerations for the frail elderly than does renting an apartment (cf. Rakoff, 1977). In part, the importance of owning a home is related to the cultural construct of independence and individualism, since Americans by and large believe these ideals are most fully enacted through the agency of home ownership.

Home owners differ from renters in the considerations they face. Objectively, the structure of Philadelphia row houses, the archetypal form of owned housing in the region, presents greater physical obstacles in the form of small size, difficult stairs, and inadequate bathrooms. With owned homes, there is no one else at all living in the building, a factor that may certainly act to reduce interaction. There are financial difficulties as well. Many of these home owners have already paid off their houses, giving them considerably lower monthly payments than renters. Yet they are responsible for repairs, utilities, and the taxes that are a part of home ownership.

Subjectively, home ownership encapsulates a cultural ideal. There is likely to be a stronger connection with the space with this more complete form of possessorship. Living a longer time in the owned home, the resident is likely to have raised or been part of a family there and to have shared this particular home with a spouse. Within this culturally idealized developmental setting, there may be a greater focus on people as an integral part of the psychological meaning of home. This is in addition to the owner's self-identification with personal investment in the house itself. In contrast, lacking the legitimacy of this culturally idealized form, a renter may be less likely to view physical aspects of the home in terms of the people who have lived there. One of our informants noted, concerning her owned home, "My husband did all the woodwork himself. He put that archway in." For obvious reasons, this is not the type of personal association usually found among renters.

Some Cases

Next, we turn to the examination of some case material about home and the meaning of home for the frail elders we interviewed.

Mrs. Annie Ford (SN)

At 90, our oldest informant, Annie Ford, was one of 18 children raised on a farm outside Philadelphia; she is the only one still living. She lives alone in a working-class neighborhood. Mrs. Ford spends most of her time on the ground floor. She is afraid of going up the stairs to the bedrooms, or down into the basement, although she does so now and then.

The front room is where she now does most of her living. This room has a hospital bed along the front wall under the window, purchased for her second husband in the last few months of his life. He passed away a little more than a year ago, and after his death she kept the bed for her own use. She had a dresser moved down into this room so that she could store her clothing there. Like many of the homes we visited, the living room now centrally functions as a bedroom and office. Mrs. Ford has all of her paperwork, medications, and important functional items neatly arranged on the shelves behind her rocking chair, the place she spends most of the day. Regardless of how poorly she may be feeling, Mrs. Ford gets herself out of bed and dressed each morning. She said, "It is not right to be in bed all day." When asked how she spends her time, she said, "Just as you found me."

Beyond the living room is the dining room, which now is used to stack and store those items that will not easily fit in the front room or that are used less often. The table had a stack of old newspapers on it, rolls of paper towels, as well as some folded sheets, towels, and clothing. A few summer dresses were hanging on the cellar door. Through the dining room was the kitchen and bathroom.

Mrs. Ford is one of the lucky few who has a bathroom on the ground floor of her home. (Most of the row houses in Philadelphia only have bathrooms upstairs.) She explained that when she first moved here 53 years ago they had no bathroom, and that her first husband added it.

The kitchen was very cluttered. Near the stove were the required items for brewing tea or coffee. The drawers were left open, so that she would not have to pull them open to get things out. The outside door to the backyard was barred, and locked with two padlocks. The yard was a small, walled, cemented area, and there were two large doghouses but no dogs. The exit to the alley behind the house was blocked by a large piece of sheet metal held in place by a stack of cinder blocks. If Mrs. Ford needed to leave through the back exit in an emergency, it would be close to impossible for her.

Mrs. Ford's strong attachment to this home is easy to comprehend only if one knows the story of how she happened to move into it. This is a story that Mrs. Ford retold during each interview without prompting. Mrs. Ford was married twice. Each marriage was distinctive. She explained that the first time she was married, it lasted "57 years, 3 months, and 2 days," and the second time "around 11 years, I guess." Any mention of the second marriage is qualified by the statement "I married for companionship. You only love once," or a similar statement.

She loved her first husband. She married him when very young and against her family's wishes. The marriage was not always idyllic. Yet, it is this love that she cherishes, and it is still very much a part of her everyday life and her sense of who she is. Many of the objects she has in the front room are mementos of him and of their marriage, and she still uses his last name. And the most important symbol of this love is the house itself. Mr. Ford was in the service during the first world war. Several years after his discharge, he received a sum of money, which, she explained, was a bonus for his war service. Mr. Ford took this money and bought the house for her. She noted, "He bought it for me so that I would always have a roof over my head. And I love it because he thought enough of me to buy it for me. My heart would be broken to leave my home." It pleases her that his wish is being fulfilled. And it pleases her that she was loved. Her home is a haven, a symbol of her first husband's love, and a symbol of the love she has given to many over the years. She concluded, "If it wasn't for my home where would I be?"

An ethos of kindness and generosity are central to Mrs. Ford's definition of herself. She noted, "I try to be kind and considerate. If possible I like to do for people. It helps my life to be kind to others. I'd like to have more friends, have more people coming in." Her home has been a place where she has been able to help and care for people throughout her life. She fondly remembers when she and Mr. Ford were a young couple and would entertain their friends at home. One of her sisters left her to care for a niece who had a clubfoot, because the sister could not afford the medical expenses. Mr. and Mrs. Ford raised this girl as their own. Mrs. Ford still keeps the casts that were put on the girl's legs as an infant. (She braved the stairs to get them to show me!) It was also in this house that she cared for both husbands through their illnesses and an elderly uncle that "everyone" had wanted to put into a nursing home.

Mrs. Ford always took great pride in the care that had enabled her to keep her uncle and first husband out of nursing homes. She promised her second husband that she would never put him in a home, but unfortunately, at 89 years old herself, she was unable to continue caring for him alone, and she finally had him admitted to a nursing home. A few days later he passed away. She regrets having had to break her promise to him.

"I had an uncle that lived with me, Uncle Keith. I was going to put him in a home, because he got bad. I took him up here to the one on Richards Road. I was gonna put him in the home up there. And, when we got there. It was winter. And, they were sitting on the benches there. Their coats were open. Their shirts were all unbuttoned. There was a women standing by a tree. She thought she was hiding herself. She had a loaf of bread, and she was eating. And, I said to Lisa, 'In the name of God. I can't put Uncle in here.' Uncle was crying. She said she'd drive on. He was crying. I was crying. Even Lisa was crying. She said to Uncle Keith, 'Uncle, we're taking you back home. We're not leaving you.'" So, Mrs. Ford cared for this uncle several years longer until he passed away.

Mrs. Ford does not even consider a nursing home as an option for herself. She is unaware of the variety of facilities available today.

White Bluff Housing Project is located on the edge of a park in the northern sector of Philadelphia. The project lies between a busy shopping area and the park itself. Across a major road from the housing project is a strip mall with a supermarket, a large hardware store, a lumber yard, a bowling alley, a discount department store, several small restaurants, delis, and fast-food establishments, as well as a variety of smaller stores. This mall is on the routes of several bus lines. This is an amenities-rich area.

White Bluff is one of the earliest public housing projects opened in the Philadelphia area. Spread over the hilly grounds are numerous buildings, arranged in garden apartment fashion. Most face courtyards or large public areas. Some of the public areas have walkways, picnic tables, or playgrounds. Except for a few buildings facing the mall across the street, most are oriented inward. The project road has offshoots that lead into cul-de-sacs and parking lots, providing access to all the buildings.

The design tends to insulate the project from the surrounding area. Buildings face one another, and everyone seems to have a view of others' front and backyards. This all serves to create the aura of a small, separate community. Residents are often visible, active in hanging out laundry, working in gardens, or fixing cars. The population is heterogeneous, including blacks, Hispanics, Asians, and whites.

Placement is based on income and family size. Residents pay one third of their income for rent, including utilities. The housing authority provides maintenance services, and grounds upkeep. There is a management office on the grounds, where residents pay their rent and which they call if their apartments need repairs. Attached to this office is the senior citizen's center, which serves a hot lunch five days a week. However, only one of our three subjects ever leaves her home, and she only irregularly attends the center's lunch. She does walk across to the mall to do her shopping. The informants were pleased with the level of upkeep and service and spoke highly of the woman who runs the office. During one interview the heat was not working in an apartment. The informant called the office, gave her first name, and they knew who she was. Within ten minutes, the heat was functioning properly. At another interview, the informant was having a new washing machine installed by a repairman from the housing project. Later, when the homemaker tried to start the machine it did not work. The informant called the office, and a different man was there in five minutes and solved the problem. Her laundry was done before the interview was over.

The three informants living in the project said they were very satisfied with their neighborhood. None of them has considered moving nor would they like to. They noted the convenience, neighborliness of fellow residents, low cost, manageable size of apartments, and personal attachment to their homes as reasons for liking the project housing. When asked what the worst things about living there were, two did not respond and the third listed a few minor changes she'd been wanting to make in her home. Overall they were very satisfied with their homes and the neighborhood. All three informants moved in at different times for different reasons.

Mrs. Edith Hines (SN)

Mrs. Hines was one of the original residents and has lived there for 51 years. During the 1930s when she was a young widow whose three children were in a foster home, she never thought she would ever be able to have her own place where she and her children could be together.

"I wanted a place of my own. And I just never felt that I could do it. Because I had disposed of all my furniture. I worked in a dress factory. And one day a shipper came in. He called me out. He said, 'Come here, come here.' He said, 'Sit down and sign this.' I said, 'Wait a minute. I'm not signing anything if I don't know what it is. What is this?' He explained about the new public housing project. A government place; they were building it; you put your application in, and rent was based on your income. I said, 'Jimmy, you know what I make. And I can't afford any place.' He said, 'I'm putting my application in, and I got one for you. You put it in. Marge and I will help you all we can. Take it and think about it.' So I thought about it. I signed it. I got in, and Jim never got in. When I got the place I thought, Now, what am I gonna do with it? Brought some old things from down home, different ones gave me things. I managed."

Mrs. Hines originally lived in a larger apartment in the project because she had three children. When her sons left home, and only she and a daughter remained, they moved to a one-bedroom apartment where she has been since.

Mrs. Amy Bruinsma

Amy Bruinsma has been in the project for 15 years. During the first years she was very active in the neighborhood and was always outside with neighbors in the courtyard, playing games, having barbecues. She was instrumental in establishing the senior center at the housing project and was its president for several years. For the past five years her health has confined her to her apartment. Mrs. Bruinsma stills feels very much a part of the community, however. This is evident in the way she interacts with the maintenance and office staff. She is very familiar with them and considers them very much a part of her life. She named the project manager in her social network. She adamantly believes that she is better off in her home, and whenever she has to go to the hospital, always fights to be released. She had moved from place to place for years with very little security and very limited resources. She stated that she was glad finally to arrive at a place that could be hers for an unlimited time, a place she could remain till the end.

Mrs. Joan Leonard (SN)

Joan Leonard moved into the housing project 11 years ago with her chronically ill husband. They had been living with a daughter. She said, "We lived with them for two years, but he was so sick. And he said to me one day, 'I would just like if it was just you and I. Do you think you could get an apartment?' So we tried and we couldn't. And, then, do you know Charlie McCue? He was the, I think he was a state senator. My daughter-in-law went to see him, and told him Daddy was very sick and he would like to be by himself. They tried all over the city to get a place. She said, 'Do you think you could get him into this place?' Within a month we were here. My husband lasted one year to the day. I'm here 11 years. Ten years alone. Soon as Daddy died, Laura wanted me to go back. I wanted to stay by myself. I'm never lonely, because there is always someone around. The telephone's always ringing."

This apartment is important to Mrs. Leonard as the place where she and her husband were together, where he wanted to be together with her. Her apartment continues to be a central stopping point for her many children, grandchildren, and great-grandchildren who live in the area. She jokes about having a revolving door installed. She enjoys both having them visit as well as having the place to herself once they have gone.

She has been confined to a wheelchair for five years now but makes full use of the space in her apartment. She likes that the apartment is manageable given her disability and income. "Now that I'm here I like it. It is easy to keep clean. It's little. My wheelchair bumps into everything and knocks the paint off, but that is beside the point. I couldn't get anything as cheap as I get here.

"I love it here. Because everybody goes out of their way [to be helpful]. They never go to the drugstore or the market [alone], they pass and say,

Do you need anything? And, even all the different types of people, they are very nice."

All our informants living in this public housing project said they were very satisfied with their neighborhood. None of them have considered moving, nor would they like to. Two of the three were not bothered by outside noise, the third only a little (her apartment was in a more central location). All three were satisfied with the privacy, convenience to services, and maintenance of the homes. None of them considered their homes a financial burden. Two of the three felt safe in their homes and neighborhood both during the day and at night. One of those two had been the victim of a break-in while she was at home asleep; the other had never been the victim of a crime. The third, whose apartment had been vandalized and burglarized during a hospital stay, did not feel safe at night in the neighborhood or in her home, but felt safe during the day.

These informants discussed the uncertainty of living in low-income urban housing and the poor public image of housing projects.

Mrs. Leonard

SN: How do you feel about living in a housing project?

JL: To tell the truth. I don't know about other projects. But when I came here 11 years ago, it was like a big country club. One of the maintenance men was here the other day to fix my door. He said, "Mrs. Leonard, you and Mr. Leonard came here the same week that I did. Wasn't it nice?" Yes it was. Well, he said it is a disaster area now. When you came here, the questions that they asked you. You had to have proof of what your income was. We never had any problems here at all. But we do now. My son said, "When you hear the cops, just get in a corner because there must be shooting around." You often hear shooting, and we never heard anything like that before. Just recently you hear it. Then you hear the cops come. Something I never did is pull the shades down, and now I do. You never know when.

SN: Are you scared?

JL: No. I say a little prayer. It goes, 'I live alone dear Lord, but have no fear because I feel your presence ever near.' I say that every night . . . But all you hear is the worst part of it. But we have some nice people. Like Mrs. Jonas, she did for everybody. She didn't care whether she knew them or they were white, black, or what they were. If they were sick she took over a pot of soup, took bread. She took everything. She made everything. If people only knew the good that people do here. It is a shame.

Mrs. Hines

SN: Does it bother you that you live in a housing project?

EH: No. I guess I have no pride. People have said to me, "Don't tell them you live in a project!" I've lived here all these years, why should I be ashamed of it? It's been kind to me.

SN: How do you feel when you hear what they say about housing projects on the news?

EH: It infuriates me. Our children here are children. Children are children. But if they do anything they say, "Oh yeah, they're the kids from the project." It makes me cross. Because they are no worse, they are no better. We have plenty of nice children, and as far as I know, nice people. I don't socialize a whole lot. I'll speak to my neighbors. If I meet them I'll talk to them. I think we have some very fine people. When I was sick the neighbors came. What more could you want?

These frail elders find their housing projects full of appropriate and handy resources.

Andrew Marks (SN)

Andrew Marks, a 72-year-old retired civil servant, has lived in the same neighborhood all of his life, except for a short period in his early twenties when he was assigned to a post in Boston. Mr. Marks is very reserved; his answers to questions were very succinct and direct. He would often turn the tables in the interview, asking the interviewer the same question she had just asked him. It was only after a reciprocal dialogue was established that he began to feel at ease and his conversation became more animated.

Mr. Marks speaks with great pride about his career, his education, his financial success, and his children's success. He noted, "I worked for the government for 35 years. After, I retired. I retired not because of age but the activity I worked on moved from Philadelphia to Delaware. I went with it. I commuted; my wife didn't want to move. So I quit at 58. I got myself a job with the city for a short time. And then I got myself another job with the school district, and I stayed there 11 years.

"I got myself a degree. In business. I graduated from Temple. First, I went to the University of Pennsylvania and got an associates degree. I waited a little bit. I wasn't sure if I was going to go on. I waited a little bit then I got a degree. That was in June of 1956. That was 56 and I was born in 16. It was hard, but it was worth it. I graduated magna cum laude. It was worth it.

"My two sons went to college. Unfortunately my daughter was born too early, I guess. My middle one, my son Daniel, has a masters degree and is an executive with UTT. My other son, Joseph, he just got a PhD this year, this month, in communications. He works in New York. He's a pretty smart kid. In some ways they take after me. They're probably smarter than I am. My daughter, now she takes after me, she is very artistically inclined. She's very good with her hands, decorating, painting. You name it. She can do it. I used to do a lot of drawing, charcoal."

Mr. Marks does not see his children often, since they are all quite involved in their own careers and families. But he does speak with each of them at least several times a month. The other person to whom he is close is his brother.

At 72, Mr. Marks is able to care for himself and his home. He is still mobile, running all his own errands. He continues to manage his finances and investments actively. He has a subscription to several finance magazines. Mr. Marks is the only one of our informants who reported an income of over $50,000 per year and he noted that "money is the least of my worries."

Mr. Marks also actively manages and monitors his health. He suffers from hypertension, a recurring ulcer, arthritis, and prostate and gall bladder problems. None of these health problems are severely debilitating, yet any one could suddenly worsen. He makes an effort to get exercise and maintain a proper diet. He keeps himself informed and educated about health issues through the news and magazines.

Several months before our interviews, Mr. Marks was in the hospital. One day, he had felt tingling pain in his left shoulder. He said, "I know enough to know what that means. I took my own blood pressure and my pulse. Everything was normal. So, I just rested a bit." A few days later he felt a pain around his throat, but not in his chest, which seemed odd to him. After several days, he went to his doctor, who took a cardiogram, compared it to his most recent one, and said to him, "Don't move. You've had a heart attack. I'm sending you to the hospital." Mr. Marks was amused that, after functioning fine for several days, and then walking the five or six blocks to the doctor's office, the doctor told him not to move. He spent ten days in the hospital for tests from "all kinds of specialists."

Although he receives no assistance with activities he has had to slow down. Yet he tries to do all of his own shopping, cleaning, cooking, and laundry. The remainder of his time is spent reading, visiting his wife who is in a nursing home, and running errands. Mr. Marks has consciously included certain activities in his routine that provide the stimulation he feels is necessary. He eats lunch at a senior center to provide a bit of social contact. For exercise, he walks to buy the daily newspaper instead of having it delivered. He reads to keep himself informed and challenged.

Mr. Marks has always had a very structured routine, he concludes. Now that he is retired and alone he admits that his routine has become more important, a conscious attempt to pass and fill the time, so that he does not find himself "just staring at the walls." Life with others offers more distractions. He noted, "Conversation makes the time go so quickly. I thought I would be more amenable to living alone. But that's not true. You've gotta have some outside contact. I enjoy going out and being among different kinds of people. Young people, older people. After I retired I continued to work part-time. After a while I couldn't afford to work. By afford, I mean monetarily. All it would do is increase my taxes. So I stopped. There are times now, you know, that if I don't go to the center I don't talk to anybody all day, not saying one word except to talk to myself."

His sense of loneliness is compounded because his wife is in a nursing home. This is his greatest concern. He does not worry about his home, his finances, his health, or his children. He worries about his wife. What happens to her is the one aspect of his life over which he feels he has little control. He is deeply saddened by her pain and suffering. Their marriage, although altered, is still real for Mr. Marks. He keeps it alive. He visits her twice a week and keeps photos of her accessible. In fact he says that photos have become much more important to him during the three years she has been in the nursing home, as reminders of "happy times." He attends the same senior center that she had attended and had tried unsuccessfully to get him to attend for several years before her institutionalization.

Their home, he believes, allows him to continue to feel close to his wife although she is no longer there with him. Mr. Marks still lives in their seven room row house. The house has been maintained just as it was before his wife took ill, and he thinks of it as her house. She decorated it, she kept it up, she bought it, and she spent more time in it than he. He feels close to her there and misses her presence. He keeps a few loose snapshots of her on the kitchen counter, and he says he looks at them often. They are all very happy snapshots of her about 10 or 15 years ago.

He said, "This house meant a lot to my wife. Her father remodeled it. He was a carpenter. He was very good. Everything you see here, she arranged. The cabinets, paneling, everything." They married very young; he was 20. They were both from the neighborhood. While he was assigned to Boston for several years, his wife remained in Philadelphia. It was during his absence that she selected and purchased their home. She chose it because it was the neighborhood they had both grown up in and to both families. As Mr. Marks tells the story, his wife made all of the arrangements for the purchase. And, then she had the house renovated to her tastes. He noted, "The special meaning this home has to me is that its the place that we started. Where we did a lot of things together. Personal relationships took place here. My kids were here."

As Mr. Marks discussed the meanings his home has for him, regrets came to mind. He noted "some of the things I did that I shouldn't have. Like I worked too hard. But I had to." He regrets not spending more time with his wife and family when they were here. And of his home he noted, "It's just that I am here. It is a place to be. I guess you could say it's a haven.

"Most of my life has been here. You can't live in a place all this time and not feel some affinity for it. I could leave it, though. What's to keep me here? It wouldn't bother me that I left here. At least that's the way I feel. That may turn out to be wrong, but that's the way I feel right now.

"The neighborhood is changing here. There is no question about that, although it hasn't done so completely. For example, on the next block that way, I'm trying to think if there are any Asians there now. Not that they bother me. They don't bother me. But the next block, it's turning Asian, there are an awful lot of Asians. But it's not a cause for worry.

"I'll tell you one thing that has been happening. There is someone. I can't imagine why. Every once and a while they will throw an egg against my facade of my house. I don't even know who's doing it. And I have no idea why. That annoys me very much. I wish I could get my hands on whoever it is.

"I guess the best thing about living here is the familiarity with my surrounding. For example, the center is close by. I could walk to it. The bank is close by. I could walk to it. I have a car, but I keep it in the garage. I need the exercise for one thing. Everything is around here. And I am so familiar with it it's like second nature. The only fly in the ointment is what's happened. It doesn't happen often, but every time I let my guard down about looking out the window, it happens.

"It would only bother me a little to leave my home. Because I would be leaving something that I was so familiar with all these years. It's the familiarity. Let's face it, the neighbors, I'm not that friendly with the neighbors. There is nothing there to keep me here. You know. Some people get to know their close neighbors very well. I'm not that way. She [his wife] was, she was a very open type person. I kind of kept to myself.

"I have to say that this is home. It's not just a place to flop. Family, all the memories, things that we did here, kids. It's comfortable. It's familiar."

Mr. and Mrs. Marks had been considering moving, "before she got sick. She wanted to. Florida or somewhere else. I felt the Northeast, but for some reason she was reluctant. But that never came to fruition." If he had moved he would have missed "the convenience of knowing where every-thing is. Where every store is and that kind of thing. It would take some getting used to, adapting to another neighborhood."

Mrs. Maggie Turner (JCK)

Age 77, Mrs. Turner suffers from heart disease, chronic shortness of breath, and incontinence. She lives in a row house in an ethnically chang-ing neighborhood where long-time residents are dying off and moving out, although her neighbor on one side is also a long-time resident. The neighbors on the other side, newcomers, apparently do not work much, stay up all night, and then sleep late. Mrs. Turner believes that these neighbors use or sell drugs.

Although Mrs. Turner had no children of her own and was an only child herself, she enjoyed the company of neighborhood children as an adult. These children have now grown up and moved on and she has grown frailer. It is apparent that she misses this interaction. She also misses her aunt-in-law, whom she cared for in her final years and who willed her the house in which she now resides. When Mrs. Turner's husband died, the aunt-in-law asked her to move in with her and she did so. Having no place of her own and not working, she agreed. She did not see this as a burden, she noted, because her aunt-in-law, although bedrid-den, had such a pleasant personality.

Her parents died when she was young. Although she has an uncle in his nineties who lives in Florida, in her words, he has "one cane in the grave." Her best friend of 27 years died a week prior to our interviews. Mrs. Turner described at length the fun they used to have together and how much she misses her. Lacking children, Mrs. Turner expressed con-cern about to whom she will leave her belongings when she passes away.

Television is the major source of her daily activity. She goes to bed at 12:00, after "Nightline." Although she has shortness of breath and had a heart attack a few years back, she still sleeps in one of the three upstairs bedrooms. But the climb is becoming more and more difficult and she foresees having a hospital bed downstairs eventually, if she can afford it. Her income is limited to Social Security of around $430 a month. She also receives food stamps and meals-on-wheels. When she needs to travel, she takes cabs rather than elder transport, since the cabs are more reliable and she fears incontinence in public places. This fear keeps her almost a prisoner in her own home.

When the interview was conducted, Mrs. Turner and the interviewer sat in her dining room; the living room is unusable. Mrs. Turner has been waiting for someone from the city to come and fix the ceiling of her living room. Her home needs structural repair, but because she does not have the money, she must wait for the city to send someone at a reduced rate. In the living room a large portion of the ceiling has recently fallen down from a leak in her bathroom that occurred years ago. She has been waiting for quite some time for city personnel to come and fix it. She says that meanwhile she can no longer have neighborhood children visit to play cards because she is afraid that pieces of the ceiling that occasionally fall might drop on them and hurt them. She hopes none falls on her while she is on the couch watching TV. During several months of contact with this informant, the ceiling still had not been repaired. This repair-to-be had been initiated by her previous social worker about whom Mrs. Turner spoke with respect and affection. Unfortunately, the social worker had quit her job, and Mrs. Turner was waiting to meet her replacement.

Mrs. Turner was first married in her early twenties, but for only two years. Her husband, who liked to ride motorcycles, stepped on a nail, she said, and she believes the hospital did not treat him correctly because he died from the infection! She married her second husband in her fifties after he had been married for some 20 years and divorced. She had dated him before she got married and she just happened to bump into him again after his divorce. He was a taxi driver who never believed in saving money, she said. She cared for her husband during a lengthy illness until he died and then for her husband's aunt.

Now, from this, she has a home of her own although it did not come with the family she always longed for. Her parents died young and her earliest recollections are of foster homes. She had difficulty remembering the names of families and the situations. She did, however, recount to the interviewer tragic instances of childhood abuse. Of her life she said, understandably, "I had a poor life and I never had anything and I tried to work and do well. It wasn't a happy life but I made the best of it."

While most of what she views as negative changes in the neighborhood can be left outside her door, some cannot. She lives in a changing neighborhood where older neighbors are dying or moving out as younger families with different customs arrive. Most disturbing to her, however, is that a family who may be dealing drugs has moved in right next door. A lot of young people go up their back stairs from the alleyway all hours of the night and early morning. The woman there does not live with her husband and all kinds of people are running in and out all the time. The woman claims they are her cousins. Of her neighbor, Mrs. Turner noted, "Oh, she used to scream and holler. She'd break everything, throw everything out there in the alley, her furniture. The racket they made! You can see her furniture laying out there. And break her windows. Her doors were broken off so many times."

The interviewer noted that it appeared quiet now, and Mrs. Turner said that they sleep late during the day. However, shortly thereafter the neighbors woke up. This was about 12:30. Doors slammed and objects banged against the wall. They could be heard yelling angrily at each other and their voices coming from next door were clearly audible in the tape recording of the interview made in Mrs. Turner's home. Mrs. Turner's hands began to shake as we continued our interview. She had no knowledge of what these crazy people might do sometime in the future. She felt the fear of the unknown.

Later, when asked whether she liked her home, Mrs. Turner replied with a tentative "Yeah." But when asked if it were special to her she said, "Well let's say that I never had a home of my own. It's mine and I want to keep it until I die." She fears going to a nursing home since this is where her best friend died a week before our interviews.

She said, "I never want to leave this house. I mean if I was so sick I'd get the lawyer and tell him, 'Keep me in this house. Don't take me out to a nursing home I'd die.' I'd want to die before I'd go to a nursing home. This home is mine and I want to keep it until I die." She never thought that she would own her own home since whatever money she had was absorbed by medical bills. Now that she finally has one, she chooses to stay in it because it is the one possession she has that is meaningful to her and makes her feel a part of life.

Again, these cases illustrate the conflicting nature of individualism and collective responsibility. As a cultural symbol of individualism, the home is increasingly troubled by an outside world that does not necessarily stop at the doorstep. And pain that is experienced privately is not necessarily an object of community interest or care. Further, stigma attached to the public housing identity was perceived by our informants as unfortunate and inaccurate. In most cases, a supportive dimension of community life was absent or neglected. As the case of Mr. Marks illustrates, many elders feel that much is incumbent on them, as individuals; this is true even when capacities are greatly limited.

5

The Effect of Life History on Individual Choice: The Nature and Role of Continuity

A very great deal of recent theoretical work in gerontology has examined the nature and role of continuity in defining and maintaining the self in later life. This work has viewed the making and maintaining of identity as central but problematic. Continuity is contingent on confronting the variety of profound changes that come with age.

In this chapter, we explore the relationship of continuity in personal identity to the enactment of choice, given the presence of frailty and health problems. (In so doing, we again identify the role of home in this process.) The existence of multiple or severe health problems, both objectively and subjectively, limits and shapes the choices that people feel they have and are able to make. This profile of choices is itself dependent on the form that people attribute to their lives and to their identities. And this in turn is contingent on those aspects of identity that individuals have selectively emphasized and sought to maintain throughout the lifetime. Certainly, the onset of sudden illness or health difficulties affects the maintenance of continuity of identity insofar as identity has been defined with specific respect to those domains directly affected by health concerns.

A sense of identity is shaped both by social and cultural concerns and by personal ones. Identity is both static and malleable. A person's sense of identity may contain a "core," or a central issue or problem to which many of life's activities, no matter how diverse, are ultimately directed. Or an identity may be more diffuse and incorporate several issues. One good way of understanding personal identity is in the life history, or the story of the life that one narrates to a listener. This story is pitched backward in time. In essence, it is a representation of the past, on a chronological or other basis, in the present. But it is always important to remember that all life histories are present-day constructs. They do not represent "the truth." Rather, they are historically constructed narratives shaped by current and present-day issues.

As we have shown so far, and particularly in Chapter 4, both life history and the emotions and experience of home are meshed closely. In a sense, one's life history and residential profile are representations of one another. As our elderly informants have indicated, when one has lived 20, 30, 40, or more years in the same place, there is a fine degree of articulation between person and place, an ease, comfort, interconnectedness that is profound and is both ideational and behavioral. People and their places are close and are part of one another.

Older people, frail or not, face issues of constructing a sense of lifelong continuity and coherence. In general, there can be two sorts of ways in which continuity of identity can be constructed. First, personal continuity can be built into a larger, external system of continuity making. That is, by simply being a certain type of person or by normatively playing certain roles or existing in certain contexts, continuity of identity is socially ensured. Here, continuity is dependent on some external condition socially defined as unchanging. An example of this is the identity one obtains by being a member of the family into which one was born. While the Smith family may be famous or interesting for the deeds performed by certain of its members, this corporate identity is shared by its component individuals by virtue of birth rather than performance. Thus continuity by life structure or role (that facilitated by those orienting circumstances external to the person that motivate aspects of continuity) includes elements such as health status and aspects of life structure such as class and life expectations. And continuity through social categories includes the basic orienting elements of social identity such as race, religion, and gender. Although what it means to be a woman, for example, may change with age, historical period, and health status, one always is a woman.

In contrast, the establishment or maintenance of continuity of identity may require active achievement. That is, rather than being part of "the system" of identity making, it is incumbent on individuals to build or make their own sense of personal continuity ("I have always loved nature" or the like). Achievement of identity is an important part of American adult life.

In both types of continuity, the person may have cause to reinterpret or re-emphasize aspects of past life history to fit present-day circumstances. There are many media of continuity, which are symbolic constructions that help maintain continuity of identity through some other sphere of being that stands for aspects of selfhood. As we have seen in the previous chapter, housing can provide one important form of continuity. As the body is increasingly threatened, the significance of staying in place for maintenance of continuity also increases.

Besides continuity of identity created through the maintenance of life space, we may distinguish other domains of such a symbolic construction. Personal themes, or habitual ways of referencing the self, are broadly applicable to a variety of life circumstances, are symbolically manipulable, and can create continuity through their ability symbolically to condense disparate happenings in life into a single type of named, overarching, thematic experience (Kaufman, 1981, 1986).

The cases presented in this chapter emphasize continuity of personal identity and demonstrate how such continuity is transferred into the domain of choice making, given the circumstances of frailty. If poor health or physical handicap has been part of a person's identity at an early age, and one has in some way successfully adapted to it, later life adaptations to small changes in health status may be less threatening to self-image or continuity than for someone who has not experienced health problems until later life. For some, the expression of this continuity may be varied or unclear at first glance, but in each case we will highlight and narrate the nature of the continuity of identity as we conceive of it. We begin with the case of Etta Cohen.

Mrs. Etta Cohen (SN)

The only child of parents she remembers as "strict but fair Pennsylvania Dutch," Mrs. Cohen remembers most vividly the things about her family and childhood that were different from those of her peers. All of her friends' mothers were younger, more lively, more fun than her own, who was already in her forties when Mrs. Cohen was born. She was not allowed to dress like the other girls, climb trees or fences, nor be spontaneous and affectionate. She credits this strict upbringing with teaching her responsibility for her own choices and actions: "I had a good childhood. I wasn't allowed to do some of the things that the other kids did, but my mother did it for my own good. I deserved every one of the lickins I got." In retrospect, she views the early experience of being controlled as positive.

After high school, Mrs. Cohen's mother sent her to Philadelphia to attend business school to acquire a useful skill. She never quite understood her mother's motivation in this decision. She noted, "My mother was trying to raise a lady. Why she sent me off to Philadelphia right after graduation, I'm not sure." Suddenly Mrs. Cohen found herself able to make her own choices free of her mother's often subtle, yet always present, judgment, a sense of freedom she valued. She characterizes this period of her life as her "Philadelphia freedom experience." She lived in a Lutheran boardinghouse for girls and did everything young women in boarding houses do: gossiped, went out, bought clothes, snuck out to meet boyfriends. She said, "The Philadelphia experience at the beginning was more of a freedom thing for me. I saw things that I had never seen before . . . I got the first freedom, I got a taste of freedom. I could go when I wanted to go. I could stay home when I wanted. I liked the fun in Philadelphia."

She remembers deliberately engaging in activities of which her mother would not have approved or even understood: "I used to mention cocktails in my letters home to my mother and, God rest her soul, she did not know what a cocktail was, and when I went home for a holiday my mother bought cans of fruit cocktail, and when I said, 'Mother, I don't like that,' and she said, 'But you eat them all the time in Philadelphia.' Well, I had to tell her that, what I ate, I didn't eat, I drank . . . I feel a little guilty about this." She continued, "I bought, much to my mother's disgust, I bought my clothes on time. I had a charge account at Strawbridge's [a department store]. By the time the clothes were worn out I still hadn't paid for them. My mother never bought anything on credit like that."

This was a very active, varied period in Mrs. Cohen's life. She went from job to job, apartment to apartment. Her social life was busy and diverse. When discussing the places she lived, worked, and played, she would always locate them very specifically, often by address.

Mrs. Cohen's first marriage was subsumed by her narration of this early period of her life. She said of her first husband, "He was a friend from that time." She continued to move around with him as he changed jobs. In fact, these were the only residences that she was not able to remember in detail. This marriage was brief, and appeared inconsequential in the telling of her life story. The pace of her life slowed after her first marriage. Jobs and apartments began to last longer. Yet, the diversity continued. Career shifts were no longer merely from one secretarial position to another: Instead she went from retail sales to keypunching, to child care, to operating machinery in a ball bearing factory.

It was around this time, between her two marriages, that her parents passed away. Her father had been ill for quite some time, and died of a stroke while her mother was here in Philadelphia caring for Mrs. Cohen after an appendectomy. Her mother tried to persuade her to return home: "When my father died, my mother wanted me to come back. She would have gotten me a job. And she said she would buy me a car. She said, 'Well what can you do in Philadelphia that you can't do here?' I said,'I can do anything I want to in Philadelphia. If I don't want to do it, I don't have to, but when I want to do it, it's there.' She said, 'In other words, you'd rather have two dimes in Philadelphia than a bank account back home.' That's right!"

Mrs. Cohen married a second time at age 35. Her second husband was also divorced and had a son with whom he had lost contact. The fact that her husband Fred was Jewish was and continues to be an important element in her life. She made it known before the marriage that she would not "turn for him," but throughout her marriage she made an attempt to respect his family's religious beliefs. She would always observe any dietary restrictions when she had her in-laws over for dinner. Today, it is the Christian holidays that are the loneliest for her. Her obviously Jewish last name has allowed her passively to permit others to believe her to be Jewish in situations where that would benefit her.

Mrs. Cohen worked for the first six years of this marriage until health problems forced her to stop. She was in her early forties. For the first few years of their marriage Etta and Fred lived in two rooms of his family's home. That arrangement became tense, so they moved to an apartment of their own. "And then Fred saw this house up here, and he liked it. And he decided that we should move. I had never lived in a house, you know. I'd lived in boardinghouses, I'd lived in an apartment. But, when I'd thought about coming up here, this house looked like Rockefeller's building, it was so big. I had just gotten over a gall bladder operation, and I just wasn't for this house at all. I didn't even have any interest in going downtown with him to buy the furniture."

It took Etta Cohen some time to get used to her new home. "I just wasn't accustomed to who I was living around . . . I just wasn't accustomed to having somebody right in my front door, you know what I mean? Before, I was on the third floor at my mother-in-law's house. Then Fred started fixing the new home up. We changed the, we took doors off there and put arches. And, we painted. We put tile floors. We made improvements. It was no drastic change in the house. Except that we made it more comfortable . . . I didn't care for it here, and then when I got to know the people . . . I talked to the different neighbors, then I started to like it."

When asked if her home is the center of her world, Mrs. Cohen replied, "It wasn't at one time. It was the core but I had a lot of spokes going out from it. I was always glad to get back to my home.

"This place is worth, this place is worth . . . I would say it is worth just about everything I have. First of all, my husband's lifeblood was put in this house. He made the, he painted walls, he tore out partitions, and put arches in. And he always kept everything nice. He would turn over in his grave, as dead as he is, he would turn over in his grave if he would see what is going on around here in this neighborhood. This house means an awful lot to me. It is the best place for my morale, but definitely not the best place for my whole body. The trouble that I have physically is not going to improve with dampness, like in here. That isn't helping my condition any, I know that."

She added, "I'm very comfortable here. It has always, no matter when I have come back. Sometimes in the wintertime I would be sitting out at the table, I sit there in the chair next to the refrigerator. And I would look in here and the soft lights were on, in wintertime you know, and I had my heavy drapes up. I have like gold color drapes that go up there in the wintertime. And the light there, and little sparkly things around that I had. I used to sit out in the kitchen and I'd look in, Oh, that room looks pretty. The gold drapes did make a big difference. I always had my cover on the davenport. I used to say, Gee, I've got a pretty little home."

Forty years after moving into this home, Mrs. Cohen had become so attached to it that she resisted being forced out by the city, who wanted her to move. She had lived in this space for 40 years, 20 with Fred and then 20 alone after he died. She could not imagine living anywhere else; this place, she said, was her life. Listening to Mrs. Cohen speak about her past, as well as her present routine, it was often difficult to distinguish where, or even if, she and her home were two separate entities.

"Fred was sick the last three or four years that he lived. He was sick without knowing why, he was a big man, and he kept getting thinner and thinner and thinner. And then his feet got to the point where he couldn't walk any more, then he went to the doctor. That's what they found diabetes, so from then on in he worked, but then he would fall asleep . . . He was endangering himself. They told him they couldn't use him any more, and he came home a broken man. That was in October, and by January he was in the hospital and that was the end."

Fred's condition worsened. He began to fall often and became increasingly disoriented. He stopped recognizing people. He had been a jeweler all his life and during the last few months of his life he would sit at the table and act out the motions of making jewelry. Mrs. Cohen remembers this with sadness and empathizes with Fred. She knows the embarrassment he would have felt, had he been aware of his behavior. Confident that she herself can adapt to any physical or social limitations that aging may bring, it is only the thought of losing her "mental faculties" that terrifies Mrs. Cohen.

When Fred passed away, the neighborhood had already begun to change. Friends and relatives suggested that she move into a smaller place, perhaps an apartment. But by this time, her 20 years in her home had fostered a complex attachment to the neighborhood, the house, and the experiences she had had in both. Even if she had been willing to move, her finances would have prevented it. This was before widows began to receive their husbands' pensions, she noted, and unfortunately Fred had never "believed in" life insurance. So, Mrs. Cohen stayed.

She said, "Being alone in this home has never bothered me that much. Now, there are two thoughts on that. One is loneliness, the missing of other people around you. And being alone that's different, different altogether. Now, being alone has never bothered me because I have been alone all my life. Loneliness is another thing. But being alone, the fact that I had to live here alone did not bother me. But I did not know how long I would feel Fred's presence, you know what I mean. Some people can't live in a place after their loved ones are gone. If they are by themselves they can't live that way.

"But, you must remember, I was an only child, and my mother was 41 when I was born, so I grew up with an older generation. All the kids that were in school with me their mothers were 23, 24, 25 years old. My mother was 41. Then when I first came to Philadelphia I lived with 21 girls but I had my own room. I was friendly with all of them but we didn't have any close relationships. We went out together . . . But I always was glad to go upstairs and close the door, and either read a book or close the light off and go to sleep. After I moved away from there I moved into an apartment by myself.

"I can keep myself. All my life I played alone. I was alone with everybody, with everybody I was alone. So I was inside of me. It's a heck of a way to explain something but. Oftentimes people say, 'I don't see how you stay here by yourself.' I'll be more alone where I move to then I would ever be here. But as far as being lonely for people, I am not. I enjoy having someone come in, if someone would come in and sit down, we'd talk. I like to hear about what is going on in the outside world."

At first glance, the sense of continuity portrayed by Mrs. Cohen may not be obvious, since her life appears to have little topical continuity. However, there are two very important forms of continuity displayed both in the content of her story and in the way in which she has chosen to explicate it.

The first form of continuity is seen in the theme of adaptability, constructed from a variety of disparate materials. From the perspective of her current life, she portrays herself as someone who had adapted, as a youth, to situations both of restricted freedom and choices and of greater liberation; she has survived a bad marriage and adjusted to loss in a good one; she sees continuity in her present-day life-style and aloneness with the fact that she was an only child of older parents. She is and views herself as supremely adaptable, for any state, up to the point of cognitive deterioration.

The second aspect of continuity is concentrated in her love of and sense of attachment to her home. It emotionally and physically embodies who she is now. It enabled a located sense of continuity to the life she shared with her husband to develop, and enables her, to a degree, to overlook the profound neighborhood changes around her.

More recently Mrs. Cohen has been faced with the new challenge of creating a life that enables her to live with the physical limitations of age. She is severely afflicted by both rheumatoid and osteoarthritis, drastically limiting her mobility, making walking, reaching, bending, sitting, and even sleeping uncomfortable, if not painful.

"My age is against me. You have got to realize that after a certain age, you are not as active and can't be as active, especially crippled with arthritis as I am. You see how I have to walk. Now, I can do without this cane in the house. I don't do it, but I can. I can't straighten up. When I'm sitting in a chair, no one would know there was anything wrong with me. Then I get up and start to walk all bent over, because right here at the base of my spine I have arthritis, then it runs into the hip, especially my right one . . . I can move my legs while I am here . . . but when I go to get up on my feet that's a different story.

"There are days when I don't want to get out of bed. The mornings are not without tears.

"I don't know how I got to be 83 almost, but somewhere along the line I grew up. I had never thought of myself as an old person until this thing [gestured to large water spot on the living room wall] happened. Then I had realized that age has an awful lot to do with your ailments and your attitude. I used to see elderly people; all I can remember about elderly people is that they complained that they were so nervous or they couldn't do this or they couldn't do that. And, I used to say, If they wanted to do it they could do it. Well, I find *they* can't. No matter how much I want to do some things, I can't. I try to make it as convenient for myself as I can. So that the things that are the hardest for me to do, I leave until the very last minute . . . And if I have any energy left, I dust.

"The changes came gradually. It didn't happen overnight. It took a long time for these legs to get to the point that I had to give things up."

Mrs. Cohen gradually changed her routine in order to accommodate her frailty. She used to walk everywhere to do her shopping, carrying her parcels back home. She even told of walking several blocks to purchase a Christmas tree and lugging it home on a cart. She said, "It started getting real bad, I could still go a year ago. No, not a year ago I couldn't. About a year and a half ago I could still walk down here to the avenue and get on the 34 Bus and get off at Cole Street, that was where the doctor was and the grocery and all, and since they delivered the groceries, I didn't have to carry anything home. They would bring it. Then I'd get back on the bus, which was right outside of the store. But, after that, I began to get to the point where, by waiting the 20 or 25 minutes that I had to wait for the bus . . . They did have at one time have a place where you could sit over there and wait, but the kids tore all the benches up. So there was no place to sit, and I had to stand. If I went up on the doctor's steps, then I couldn't see the bus as it was coming, and I couldn't run for it. If they would have come over to the curb, it wouldn't have been a problem, because the old buses had a handle on each door. I could grab that handle and pull myself up, but these newer buses that they have, they're a different thing all together, you have no place to grab. And see, I must pull myself." When Mrs. Cohen could no longer manage the buses, she began placing her grocery order by phone. She now relies on the inconvenient and uncertain services of her brother-in-law and a young woman who delivers her meals, to drive her places.

Mrs. Cohen has also made adjustments in her routine inside as well as outside the home. She now pays all her bills by check, takes care of most of her business by phone, receives meals from Aides to Friends. She has constructed rigid daily and weekly routines that center on the essential care of herself, her house, and her cat. The television, radio, newspaper, and crossword puzzle have become her major sources of entertainment and access to the outside world.

Of this routine, she noted, "Since I am like I am, I try to do the laundry at least once a week. But sometimes, I can't always, it all depends on the season of the year. When I have extra pieces, like extra little sheet blankets or something like that to wash, it means that I can only do the clothing. And since my washer is 20 some years old down there, I try not to overload it. It is a large capacity. I can put a full bedding, sheets and pillowcases. I sleep on three pillows. That's probably partially because of my back. I can't lay perfectly flat. I have undercovers, I don't do them once a week but I do them once a month. So that makes a fairly good load, the two sheets and the six pillowcases. And then if I have any small pieces of my own, like brassieres or panties, I can throw those in with that. The larger pieces, like my house dresses and things like that, they have to go in with the towels. I used to do two loads in one day.

"Now, see, I don't have a drier, just a washer. And, I have five lines in the cellar that I hang my clothes on. Right now it is almost impossible for me to hang them. I have to grab a hold of the line this way, and hold on to it so that I can get it. Because I can't get my arms up. When I do it pinches me right across here. I can hang maybe five small pieces and then I have to sit. That's the way I've been doing it for, I would say, the past six months.

"If I have anything like a mattress cover to wash that's all that I do.

And, then I have a basket down there on wheels. I take it from the washer into that basket. It's practically dry when I hang it. And, then as I go along I push the basket with me. Then I hang up one end, then I pull the basket. I let it hang there till I feel like taking it down.

"I stay down in the cellar. I have a chair. I sit it right at the foot of the steps. I have one of these pillows, and I sit on that and I wait. When I first go down the cellar I put the wash in the washer. While that is washing, I take care of the cat's pans. I go down twice a day now, which I have had to lately because of the water from the rains. By the time I get the trash out, take my papers downstairs. I throw the wash down in a plastic bag. I have a big leather bag down there that I bring up.

"How do I get it upstairs? I take that as I go up the steps one step at a time and I lay it on the step ahead of me. I don't carry it in my hands. It takes me a while to get up the stairs. I have a metal hamper upstairs. Now I used to bring that down, filled with wash. I can't do it anymore, so I take the plastic bags upstairs, fill them with the wash then throw them down here. It's not been an easy thing for me to do . . . I do the best I can, that's all I can say. It is an effort, but I suppose, medically, they would say it was good for me, because it makes me do something. It gives me an opportunity to use my arms.

"How I get down the cellar steps? Before I go down, I throw my cane down, and I throw whatever I have to take down there down. Then I pull that chair that is right near the cellar door. I pull that over, and as I step down, I go down backwards. For the first couple of steps until I can reach the railing with my right hand I go down with my hands on the steps. Then when I reach the railing I hold onto the railing and go down the rest of the way.

"Now, coming up I bring my cane up with me. I put the cane on the step ahead of me, hand on the railing, this foot goes on it, then I drag this leg up. When I get to where the railing ends, I take my cane and I hook it over the bottom rung of that chair. Then I've got both hands free, and put my hands on the step ahead. When I get near enough, I grip the first rung of the chair. My cane is already up here. I pull myself up, and I push the chair. As I am pulling myself up the chair goes ahead of me as a walker would do.

"Once a month I have been able to switch my mattress. I don't do it any oftener then that. But I have a single bed and I have learned how to turn it. Cleaning is my hardest job. When I go to go under things I have to make two or three stabs at it. I sit down for maybe 15 minutes. Then I get up again, start over again, and I finish. I just have to live every day as it comes. When the day is gone, go to bed and forget about it. Get up the next morning and start over again. It's a heck of a way to have to live."

Mrs. Cohen's disability colors her narration of places and objects. When describing shopping trips, stores were portrayed by the physical obstacles they present: one has slippery floors, another's aisles are too long, lights too bright, shelves too high. A certain restaurant is favored because of its wide chairs with arms. Only people who have cars with movable seats are asked to give her rides. The cellar steps are compared to her main steps by the criteria of pitch and step width.

"It was just about two years before my husband died that the first black family moved into the street, two doors down the street, and they were very nice people. It was strictly a Jewish neighborhood when we moved in here. And then the blacks got in and then the people from Korea and places like that, then they started coming in, and then the neighborhood changed. Many of the people were old and they died, but the younger people, while they could still, when the children grew up and married and they moved to different sections of the city, and saw the difference between them, then they got afraid to let their parents stay here. That's what really happened. Then they would say, 'Mom, if you don't move, then we won't come see you.' So they moved out. And well, there wasn't any way to discriminate, so whoever had the money, What the hell? And those that left them to be rented. They were sorry that they did because the destruction was terrible. It was better that they sell."

The houses in her neighborhood were built over a creek bed. Insufficient and inadequate landfill was used at the time of construction. Eventually the houses began to shift and sink. Many homes' foundations were affected. In the late 1980s the city informed the residents that, due to the houses uninhabitability, they would have to relocate. Some residents did so immediately, while it took longer for others. The emigration from the neighborhood quickened the process of deterioration, as homes were left vacant and became subject to fire, vandalism, and occupation by squatters, homeless, and drug dealers.

In 1990, Mrs. Cohen was still in her home, one of the last residents left on her block. The majority of the homes were vacant, boarded up, and severely vandalized. Several had been burnt until all that remained were charred shells. She witnessed the decay of her street and her neighborhood. She watched as houses were vacated, occupied by vagrants and transients, as each house was broken into and stripped of its fixtures, doors, windows, piping, and anything else of value. She knew which of the houses were crack houses and who their regular customers were. In one interview, Mrs. Cohen spoke of watching the drug users walk past her house to make their purchases, and more often than not they would duck into one of the vacant houses on their way back, "to shoot the stuff inside of them, smoke it, or whatever it is they do." This had become so commonplace that one or two of them even greeted her if she was on the porch.

"My friends wouldn't dare come here. God forbid they might get contaminated [laughs]. They'll say, 'How do you stay there? How do you live in that house day after day, day after day? All you do is look across the street.' I have news for you. *I don't see those houses across the street.* In my mind's eye those are the houses that I've seen for 40 years, and that's the way I look at them. I remember the people that used to live there. I remember how it used to be in the summertime, and all like that. And, I'm sad about it because the death of a street is as serious as the death of a person.

"There must be other people in this neighborhood mess that I'm in. I'm only talking about this neighborhood now, because all the other sections of the city I don't know anything about. I only know what we are going through right here. I know that there are some elderly people, regardless of race, color, or creed, they're still elderly and they are still human beings. And they're still people who are grieving inside for their homes the same as I grieved, and am still grieving for it. Because if they could pick this house up and move it somewhere and sit it on another lot, I would rather have that."

Mrs. Cohen knows that she must move out of this home, yet she is hesitant and scared: "I am sitting on a keg of dynamite here." She feels this is no longer the best place for her health. The dampness is not helping her arthritis. She must bail water out of the basement whenever it rains. She once fractured her ribs doing so. The stairs are becoming more and more difficult to maneuver. Given the physical stress of maintaining her home, combined with the uncertainty of the neighborhood, this is no longer the best place to maintain high morale, she feels. She is becoming aware that her ethos of adaptibility may finally face some limits.

She noted, "I've always had a fairly strong mind of my own. That I get from my mother. And I have always been able to solve the problem somehow or other. This is the first one that I've run into that I haven't had a solution to much quicker than I am having one right now. See, my problem is this, one of my problems and I think it is a legitimate one. If I leave here, I have to leave here, but when I leave here, if I go into an apartment I will have to face the same problems I face here. I will have to have somebody go with me to get my groceries. I can take care of the apartment, just the same as I am taking care of here. Because Muffin [her cat] won't be in existence anymore, most of the places will not have pets. If I could get near a place where they would deliver.

"But I don't think I need an apartment. I don't need a nursing home. I'm far too good for that yet. But, what I would like to have is a place where I could have my meals and really have my laundry done . . . If the city would tell me what I was going to get for this house. Most of these places where you get your meals, they charge an awful amount to get in. And then they charge you on top of that, your monthly rent. The Neighborhood Assistance Corporation said they would send someone up here to evaluate the house, to give me a price on it. Since I was in this area, I was in line to be paid when I moved. They have never shown up. I just have to wait. Because, I am helpless. I can't go to them.

"Here I have priority. I was here first. They moved in on me. I was not an old woman with two canes that moved in. That scares me. Because, maybe I am wrong about that, but I feel that sometimes they've closed neighborhoods. They only want whatever is there. But to put an old person, I couldn't defend myself to save my life. I couldn't get up and get away from them. I'd have to have it happen. That's all.

"I don't say they can't get in here, they can. They can take a door off the hinges just as quick as a flash if they want to get in. But I just don't feel that way about this house. I lock up when I go to bed. I have bars downstairs. Most of these places have been completely gutted, so they are finished with that now. They just leave 'em alone until they fall down, or whatever they're gonna do with them. I just hesitate to go to a new neighborhood where things are just as bad as they are here.

"I should have been out of here years ago. Yes, I should have but I didn't go, and now at my age nobody wants me. When they see me they don't want me. Because at 83, maybe at 63 I would have this arthritis condition they might figure that my age it's OK, but at 83! How much longer has she got anyway? And with all these other ailments, they are not earthshaking but they are there. And, any one of them can become serious at any time: blood pressure, ulcer. Who knows when your kidney goes bad on you? Who knows when your bladder will go bad on you? And with this spinal trouble that I have and the legs, I am really a mess.

"This fear of moving didn't come to the surface until I began to get handicapped. It was there all the time, but occasionally it would show its head. But it wasn't the way it is now, because I could still do for myself. And, that was the main thing. And, now I am going to have to have someone to help me. If the condition of the street wasn't what it is, I would be only too glad to accept the help from somebody, like home care."

During the interviews the topic of moving came up constantly. It was obvious that she was attempting to come to terms with the necessity and inevitability of her move, to move her passivity to the realm of active choice making. She reads the apartment classifieds daily. She said she'd been having recurring dreams in which she was searching, hunting for something, and interpreted them as hunting for an apartment. The one thing she was consciously avoiding was calling and applying to the retirement homes that her social worker was suggesting to her. "I'm afraid of one of them accepting me," she noted. She interpreted her current life, even with poor environmental quality, as one of relative independence and, as one with objectively few choices, one that was relatively choice rich. (This is a paradox we will take up in Chapter 7.)

She continued, "I don't want to give up my independence. It's inbred. It's part of me. And I can't deliver myself to authority. What will be tough to take is to give these people my money and have them push me around. I want to keep my independence until the day I close my eyes.

"Sometimes, elderly people need help too. And, when you run into most elderly people after they've passed a certain age and they are alone, you run into bitterness, misery; they hurt here, and they hurt there, and they haven't got anybody to talk to. I know, I can say it, because I am one of them. But not everybody has my disposition. Now, there are a lot of times when, if I had my way, I would like to go out in the street and scream as loud as I could scream. Not say anything. Just scream, and get it out of me. Because, that tension that is constantly working inside, the general public doesn't see that, because I don't let them see it. Many, many times I have felt in my heart that I didn't deserve what I was getting. But if somebody says to me, 'What are you doing?' I'll say, 'I'm hanging in there.' What else am I gonna say?"

Postscript: A few months after completion of the interview, Etta Cohen began the process of applying for senior citizen housing. She sold her furniture, gave her pet cat of 14 years to the SPCA (a transfer that was certainly difficult and traumatic), and she applied and was accepted by a new facility for the aged and physically handicapped. They provide the midday meal in a dining hall, and she has a one-bedroom apartment and a weekly cleaning and laundry service.

"I went through a nasty time for a few weeks before coming here. It was getting worse, the leaking, the shooting. That did something to the thinking part of my brain. When I got here I was a wreck, couldn't even add two and two. But now with the stress off, I've gotten better. I'm one hundred percent better then when I came here. I thought I was losing my mind. I would have if I stayed any longer. I didn't know from nothing. I was so upset, so scared."

Immediately after her move, her major concern about the new facility was how she would get along with the other residents. After so many years alone she was not used to being in large groups of people. Several months later when I called to arrange a visit, our appointment had to be scheduled around the social activities in the facility. New social activities seem to have filled the time previously devoted to the routine of caring for her home.

Clearly, Mrs. Cohen's adaptability had won out over her attachment to her long-inhabited home in a decaying neighborhood. With help, she was able to pack up her belongings and move, and the quality of her life had apparently improved. Yet as we see her and listen to her self-narrative, we must be impressed with how her ability to adapt has overgrown merely the biographic—the content of her life story—and has infused the meaning her home had for her, her love of it, and her ability, under greatly limited circumstances, to continue to do for herself. For the time she was there, she chose to live there, and she was able to tune out some of the local physical degeneration. As she noted, she did not see the neighboring houses as they were, but as she once knew them. However, until the opportunity to move became clearly available, she felt as if she were choosing to continue to live in her old home. Once a choice became available, she chose that. She was able to pack up many of the symbols of what her home had been and to take them with her. She continued on in her new home.

Vito DeLuca (JCK)

Mr. DeLuca, age 65, lives on a quiet one-way street in northeast Philadelphia, in the middle of a block of brick and stucco row houses with his handicapped parking space in front. Inside, there are three bedrooms and a bath upstairs and on the first floor a living room, a dining room that is now being used as a bedroom, a half-bath, and a kitchen. It is simply furnished and neatly kept. The bills that need to be paid are on a table between his geriatric chair and the couch in the living room. On a chair in the far corner of the living room (at the foot of the 15 steps that lead to the second floor) is a change of clothing neatly folded.

Mr. DeLuca takes pride in his appearance and continues to enjoy dressing in a stylish fashion despite the arthritic pain he must endure just to get dressed. He speaks clearly in a strong voice that could be identified as Philadelphian of Italian descent.

With an annual income of about $9,000, Mr. DeLuca has several fiscal concerns. "It ain't that I ain't got a couple of dollars. I'd be lying to you, but I want to be conservative because I don't know what's going to happen tomorrow. And that's what I'm always thinking about, what's going to happen tomorrow. And if you don't have a couple of dollars, I've seen and heard too much of it."

Mr. DeLuca illustrates the case of a man who has dealt with lifelong continuing health problems. The sense of identity that has guided Mr. DeLuca's life is found in his concern with managing a chronic illness. He has had to deal with the pain and limitations of juvenile arthritis since he was 5 years old. He said, facetiously, concerning the pain of his illness, "After 60 years, you get used to it, they say." But he adds, "I got arthritis from head to toe and I got pain almost constantly." He is a man who likes to take control of his life to the extent that he is physically able. While he has undergone operations and therapy, in actuality he feels the course of his arthritis is pretty much out of his hands.

He uses canes only when needed. He relies on his geriatric chair and hospital bed when at home and his car for mobility outside the home. To help him with dressing, he also has devices, which he now rarely uses, but they nevertheless are there in case he should need them. Because climbing stairs causes him great pain, he has converted his dining room into a bedroom and has added a half-bath adjacent to it.

Mr. DeLuca is a widower of 5 years; and it is only in these last years that he has ever lived alone. As a child he lived with his parents, four older sisters, and two older brothers, both of whom are now deceased. In adulthood he continued, after the death of his father in 1960, to live with his mother. When he married, his mother continued to live with the couple until she died at age 90, some 10 years ago. His wife died only 5 years after that.

Parental love, especially that of his mother, is something he continues to treasure. In speaking of his mother, Mr. DeLuca said, "I was her pride and joy, and there was nobody like me in her eyes." He attributes this to his being the baby of the family and "sickly." Mr. DeLuca was very close to his mother and spoke of her with pride and affection. When he was asked to identify objects in his home of special significance to him, he pointed to a picture of his mother doing the *tarantella,* an energetic Italian dance popular at weddings. One of his favorite possessions is a picture of him taken when he was about age 2, "center stage," surrounded by his parents and siblings. He describes himself in it as "the chief, right in the middle. The only one with a seat."

Mr. DeLuca stated that when his mother died he had no photographs of her, but that his extended family members gave or lent him some photos, knowing how "inseparable" they had been. These now are displayed on a radiator cover in his "parlor." He explains he always had a sense of security because he knew that his mother and father loved him. At least once a week he drives to the cemetery to visit the family burial plot where his wife, mother, father, and two brothers are buried.

He has only one photograph of his wife, which was taken when they were visiting relatives in Florida. This was his first and only airplane ride and he hated it because it was not equipped to make life comfortable for a handicapped person. He and his wife married "late in life," when he was 35 and she was 40. They had no children. In part, he said, their living together came about as an act of fate precipitated when each was evicted from row houses in the same block to make way for the construction of a school. They had been friends for some time before this, having met at his sister's house. And the three of them—his wife, his mother and he— decided that they might as well all live together.

After they were all forced out of their homes at the same time, the three of them rented a house together across the street from their old home for a few months. When that house was sold, they looked for a home to buy and found his present house not far from where two of his sisters live. He found out about the house from a local newspaper and real estate agent. He and his brother-in-law then went to look at it and made an offer.

Mr. DeLuca was very fond of his wife and misses her still. "She was very good to me," he noted; she bought him his car. At present this car is an important source of independence for him. Mr. DeLuca says of it, "It's more or less company to a certain extent. Like when I want to do something by myself, I got the car." He exclaims further, "Oh, the car, if I didn't have the car, I think I'd go nuts. It's expensive and insurance is expensive but it's something that I've got that I can go out and do what I want at times. I don't do that much. Oh, I'd go crazy if I couldn't go out, even if it was just around the block once a day. If I couldn't do that I'd probably go nuts."

He and his wife used to go out to breakfast together each morning and he continues this ritual today. He talks about how he did everything with his wife, especially after his mother's death and his wife's retirement (at age 62). At that time Mr. DeLuca was already on disability. He was happy that his wife decided to retire early because they had a few years together until she died three years later.

Rather than depressing him, pleasant memories of loved ones are a comfort to him. Nevertheless, he thinks that soon he will need to find a confidant to fill the void left by his wife and mother. Although he is close to his four sisters, and they help him with household chores such as cleaning, washing, shopping, and occasional cooking, he does not feel that he can talk to them in confidence without their sharing the information with one another or perhaps taking offense. He explained "I shouldn't feel this way. I got to get somebody sooner or later. I don't know who I'm going to get. You got to have somebody to know what you got, what you don't got. It's not that I don't trust them [his sisters], but if I'm talking to you I want it to stay with you. Stuff I want to keep confidential I'm hesitating. Well, someday I'll have to do something."

With the exception of his niece and nephew-in-law who are 45 and live in New Jersey, his social network is comprised of his four sisters and a brother-in-law, all of whom are between 65 and 75 years old. Mr. DeLuca worries about their getting older, more frail, and even dying. It is difficult to think of his existence separate from that of his extended family. When asked about friends or neighbors, he said, "I don't really know too many now around here because I don't bother with too many. Nobody even comes out here half the time. I talk to the one next door when she's home. She's sickly and only comes home for a couple of days then goes away for a month or two to stay with her daughter. I talk to her on the phone once in a while."

Mr. DeLuca would go out more if he were physically able to do so without getting tired or being in too much pain. He would like to be able "to hit a taproom" or "go to a party once in a while when I'm invited out." Nevertheless, he goes on to explain, "but when you don't feel up to it, I feel like it's, you don't belong there. That's the way I feel because you can't enjoy yourself. You just don't know when you're going to get really tired. Oh, if I thought I could do it, I'd go out all the time but I don't. I'm only kidding myself and kidding the next person so I don't go for that stuff. If I feel real good, then it's a different story, very seldom I feel that good."

He has not permitted his health to force him to curtail important responsibilities such as paying his bills and going to the cemetery. In discussing these things Mr. DeLuca said, "I perk myself up to do these things. When I know I got to do something tomorrow I get myself prepared the day before. I mean you get in a frame of mind and say, I'm going to be able to do it, well you can't give up. You got to keep on pushing. When I give up you know that nothing can be done. I'm just done. But as long as there's a little breath in me, I'm going."

Continuity of identity has taken two forms for Mr. DeLuca. The first is the lifelong experience of chronic illness that has severely limited his mobility and made his days painful. While an aging body has also made it more difficult for him to cope physically on a daily basis, he has had a long history of learning how to adapt. He laments being unable to paint and do other repair jobs around his house like he used to be able to do, but throughout his life he has accepted his limitations and does what he can or seeks the help he needs from others. Because of his chronic arthritis, Mr. DeLuca has been used to receiving help throughout his life. He was not hesitant to state that he has someone come in twice a week to help him bathe. In contrast, other respondents have expressed that they would hate to get to the point where they would have to have this kind of help. (However, those that did need this service were happy to receive it.) Mr. DeLuca has had the same geriatric aide come to his house two times a week to bathe him for the past several years. She was sent after his hip operation and he kept her on at his own expense. He is fortunate to have the resources to do this. Further, unlike some informants with more recently acquired infirmities, he is knowledgeable about and desires to use health care devices to enable self-care.

The second element of continuity of identity is embodied in the certainty and inalienability of family life and participation over time and even with death. His life is, and has been, enabled by a strong degree of family support. Three sisters now take turns doing his laundry and come together once a week to clean his house. Once a week each of two sisters makes him breakfast and dinner. One comes over a few times a week with something for him to eat. They also shop for him. He gives them his list, coupons, and the money. However, he receives no financial support from anyone, saying that he would rather do without and live within his means. Even those family members who have passed away occupy a central place in his life and are memorialized in pictures in his home.

Family provides an all-encompassing sense of identity, a framework for living. Mr. DeLuca's family of reference is his family of orientation. He had no children. Significant persons of reference include spouse, parents, and siblings. Within the family context, it is also important to him to remain as independent as he realistically can. therefore, being able to live alone in his own home is a source of pride and pleasure to him.

When asked what he did for his condition or when in pain earlier in life, he replied, "I persevered. Well, I was younger. You can do things when you're younger. But when you get older it's tougher then. It's tough. But when you're younger you can work it off to a certain extent. You still got it but I used to get needles on my knees every week, I don't know for how many weeks I got that [cortisone]. I was glad to go. I thought it was helping me a little bit. I don't know whether it was helping me or not."

He anticipates that his arthritis will "progress" to the point that he will have no choice but to leave his home. Mr. DeLuca stated, "I'm hoping not. But I think it's going to get worse. That worries the hell out of me. Yes it does. If I could stay the way I am, even with the pain and aches, I'll be satisfied. Stay until I die. But I don't know. I don't. You know, I can't foresee. I can't foresee it but I think I'm going to get worse. I think it could happen overnight. I hope not, but this is what I feel and that's the thing that really bugs me. Something like that, when I can't do for myself, I can't do for myself now as much as I want to do, but I can do enough to keep going which I'm satisfied with under the conditions. That bugs the hell out of me very much."

JK: If it comes to that point do you have any idea where you might go?

VD: I keep saying I'm going to go in a nursing home but my sisters keep saying, "No, you're going to go with somebody."

JK: Do you prefer going into a nursing home?

VD: I think so, because I wouldn't want to burden nobody. How long can my sisters be around? They're older than me! They could be around much longer but you never know. How can they take care of you? You know, I'm thinking ahead.

As with most of the vulnerable elders we interviewed, Mr. DeLuca felt that being independent and able to make his own choices in daily life were particularly important for him. He noted, "I hope I can stay independent for the rest of my life. That's one thing I'm hoping for."

To him, independence is synonymous with freedom of choice. He explains, "You're free, you know, you can do what you want. You want to lay down, you lay down. You want to sleep, you sleep. If you want to go out, you go out."

Mr. DeLuca talked about his home and his feelings for it: "I love it. There's nothing like it. Like I said before, I got everything here. It's convenient. I got my refrigerator, I got food, I got the [geri-]chair, I got the hospital bed, I got my TV, things like that. Everything right here. And when I go out and watch TV someplace else, I can't enjoy it. I enjoy it right here because I can get up and take a little walk when I need to." Mr. DeLuca still remembers his old neighborhood as the best place he has ever lived because "the people were more friendly and knew one another." He also reminisces about how safe everyone felt. "You could leave your door open and you didn't have to worry about closing it. Front and the back door used to be open all the time in our home. Windows open wide especially in the summertime. Never closed them. Them days are gone."

He fears that his neighborhood is going to start "running down." A "Spanish or Puerto Rican" family moved in recently across the street and fixed up that house. He also says that there are a lot of Koreans. Since he keeps to himself, the presence of new and different types of people doesn't bother him. There's one neighborhood boy who climbs over the top of his car but he attributes his behavior to a lack of parental guidance, which he feels is very important, rather than to another cause. If he sold his house now he believes he would get his money back and then some. As Mr. DeLuca rides around the neighborhood, he sees a lot of houses for sale. He has not thought seriously about selling, because as he asked, "Where are you going to go? You see, people want you to go live with them. But I can't see it. I'm scared 'cause I heard too much and seen too much. We're a close family, don't get me wrong, but still and all living with them is a different thing."

Mr. DeLuca typifies someone whose identity encompasses lifelong adjustments to gradually worsening health problems in the context of an extended family. He stated that the love he received from his parents has served to provide him with a continued sense of well-being, belonging, and self-worth. In fact, in discussing his home, a place that now provides him with a present-day sense of well-being as well as a venue for memories, he noted, "I love it. there's nothing like it. I never thought I'd own a home, to tell you the truth. I thought my parents would live forever until I started getting older and sicker myself."

He enjoys the independence that living alone affords. While he loves his home and is very comfortable there at present, he is adaptable enough to realize that should circumstances such as health or neighborhood deteriorate, it might be necessary for him to move. Not wanting to be a burden to anyone and realizing the possible frailty of his sisters, he views a nursing home as likely. Mr. DeLuca receives help from others graciously and with a sense of humor, not dwelling on his own infirmity. Although he has had to accept help from others throughout his life, Mr. DeLuca still managed to define an ample sense of independence, which, when he was younger, was in part expressed through working. Nowadays he defines independence in terms of the ability to live alone in his own home, with the help of his sisters and others. Mr. DeLuca fears losing this independence should he ever need to live elsewhere, a choice—or lack of choice—he hopes he will never have to make. Nevertheless, he worries about his health getting worse, and dramatically so, and recognizes that his social support network is comprised of individuals themselves in the 65- to 75-year range who themselves are getting older and sicker.

Mr. DeLuca enjoys his daily routines such as breakfast outside. He affirmed that he was content in his way of life, a sensibility reflected in his affable, pleasant, joking manner. He enjoyed our interviews, noting, "I always thought that I didn't do much, but I guess I have." Because he is willing to do what he is able to and to accept his life as graciously as possible and help when needed, he continues to cope rather well with aging changes. His most difficult adjustment would be to a sudden loss of his family support network, a potential for loss of which he is quite aware. Because of his lifelong struggle with arthritis, however, he is also well aware of potential professional sources of help should he need them. And through conservative use of money in the past, he has enough to be able to pay for some of the services he may need. There has been continuity in his life by virtue of family and his lifelong coping with arthritis. In addition, being a male of Italian descent and the "baby" of the family has provided the self-acceptance and expectation by others that he should be cared for by family members while at the same time offering help to them to the best of his ability.

Margaret King (JCK)

We have noted that the existence of health problems, deteriorating economic circumstances, and the like can delimit and shape the choices people have. Mrs. King typifies such a circumstance. She is a 72-year-old woman of Irish descent who has lived for the past five years in a sprawling high-rise apartment complex in a middle-class suburb of Philadelphia. A climb up the eight flights of stairs to her fourth-floor one-bedroom apartment is impossible for her to attempt. And she does not like to use the building's elevator, which she described as "the old-fashioned kind" (in which a gate closes in the front) and which is not always in working order. This feeling of entrapment creates an image of an aging Rapunzel, without a prince. She suffers from elephantitis and her legs hurt her a lot, as they have done all her life. In 1983, she broke the femur in her right leg. She has often fallen at home and after several recent falls she was not found until the following morning. The last time she fell was some four months before our interviews. At that time, she broke some vertebrae and had a brain hemorrhage. Mrs. King explained, "That's why the front door looks like that—all scratched—because they couldn't get in the house, the medics, because nobody has a key but me. So now the manager has a key. But anyhow now, I have this Life Line system. And the terrible thing is I never wore it and kept it on the side of the walker here."

She explains that she is supposed to push the button on her unit every morning and night, to make sure it is still working. "They're very fast; they're here before you can take the next breath." The doctor insisted that she get it because she also has angina. During one interview, she spontaneously described the brain hemorrhage she had. She said, "Oh it was terrible, just terrible. And the lady who comes from church, she's what they call a Eucharistic minister, I'm Catholic. They have them go to the homes and give communion. So she came Sunday morning, and she went down right away and got the supervisor. She said, 'There's something wrong; Margaret's talking, but she's not answering me.' And here they opened the door and this place was a disgrace. This room was full of blood and I must have thrown blood on the walls and in the bedroom. And I was nude, but then afterwards—and I still never got over that—all the clothes and all the bedsheets and blanket were all full of blood, plus the fact, and this isn't very nice to mention, but we lose control of everything. And that was all over the place. And the doctor said, 'You don't do that until you die.' He said, 'I swear to God you died for a few seconds because that's the last draw when you're dying and everything lets go.' I was unconscious for five days . . . But I only fell once since September [when she had the brain hemorrhage], but before that it was constantly, every week or ten days."

By her own admission, Mrs. King's humor has given her some sense of release that has aided her through her misfortune over the years. This, for better or worse, has provided her with a life structure framework for continuity. Mrs. King rates her overall health at present to be "fair." She said "If my body would move like my head does, I'd be all right."

She reports her health problems to be a broken vertebra in her spine as a result of the fall in her apartment; cancer of the liver, which is in remission; liver and stomach problems; elephantitis (she has had 21 operations on her leg); the brain hemorrhage; poor circulation; osteoarthritis; glaucoma; cataracts; low blood pressure; nervousness; and trouble sleeping (for which she takes sleeping pills). She asked the doctor how much longer she had to live and he initially said one year, but hedged on this after looking at her reaction to this news. "I don't know what he saw in my face because then he said, 'or two.' As I was leaving the office he said 'You're going to live for ten more years.' I said, 'Who cares at this late date?'"

Uplifts and sources of strength in her life derive from her sense of humor and her attitude. She noted, "I think that I kept my sense of humor, and I think that I was willing to take what was sent to me. Don't ask me what I feel now though. [laughs] And as long as I had the kids and myself everything was beautiful. I had my mother and dad, too. But then everybody died. Now it's just the kids. And it does make you feel lost." She feels that her greatest achievement in life was having three children and so many grandchildren. She said, "That's the only way I can say I was successful.

"I think if I could get up and around, I could take a walk. Now one time when my son was here and that was last spring and I didn't have the back then, just the legs, he used to take me out. He'd take me out in the wheelchair and he'd walk me all around. Because I didn't know nothing. I didn't know which store was where. How far is the church, so he brought me all around, which was great. But I think if I could walk that is what I'd love to do, take a walk and see things for myself.

"The only thing I miss is being with my grandchildren. And I don't see them as often because their mothers and fathers have to work. You know it takes two now. I miss them. When I lived in the suburbs we were close because they lived nearby. And when the kids got a certain age they could walk up. The school was close to me and everyday the bus would pass and my granddaughter would say 'Mom Mom, be out on that porch at three o'clock.' And I was watching a story that ended at three. And after a couple of months of being out there, I said to her, 'I'll be out there at five after three because I don't know what's happening with all my story; the best thing is the last thing.' I'd be out there and she'd say, 'Mom Mom' and then the whole bus would say 'Mom Mom' and before you'd know it the bus driver would open the door and say, 'Hi, Mom.' But I really loved them and I always minded them to let my sons go on vacation and things like that."

She added, "I'd love to cook a big meal. And that's one thing I miss terrible is having the kids for the holiday. Well, last year wasn't so hot, but this year was the worst Christmas I ever had. I didn't go no place. I didn't go to anyone's house. I don't like people to feel sorry. I didn't have anything to eat even though the girls, my daughter-in-laws are wonderful. They wanted me to come down and, in fact, at night my son brought me in a big platter of cold turkey, but it wasn't any good as far as I was concerned because I had to eat it alone. And that's another thing. I hate eating by myself. Even when I was able to cook, I'd cook things that were fast like french fries, you know, stuck it in the oven. I didn't mess around with it because it was just me. But I can't kneel down and I can just about sit down. The thing is I can't stand up. I could feed myself. Oh I do, but all I eat is sandwiches and pizza, because I can't stand up long enough to make something."

Her lack of mobility precludes her from participating in most activities. She said, "I can't go out. Once in a while my oldest son will bring me to his house, but I'm too uncomfortable to do that much now. You can't sit right in the middle of teenagers; they have dates coming in. That's why I always said I would never live with them. I'm going into a nursing home when it's my time. And much as I would hate it, I guess. But still I would never live with them and put that burden on them. And they know it. I said positively no. Anyhow, I think they'll respect my wishes for it." Many of the informants expressed the same concern: not wanting to be a burden. While some consider nursing homes as an alternative, this is not considered without a good deal of fear.

She's been at her current apartment for five years, and it is a source of comfort to her knowing that she has a roof over her head and is settled, Mrs. King does not feel emotionally close to her home and describes it as "just a place" rather than a home. She said that it would not bother her at all to move from this apartment, if she had the help. Her restricted mobility is the main reason she dislikes this apartment. She has been on a waiting list for HUD subsidized housing for several years. There is a modern apartment complex for the handicapped in a nearby town that she would like to move into. Further, she has complaints about the building, the neighborhood, and its inhabitant that no doubt also have influenced her attitude to her apartment.

Her doctor's office is the only place she now regularly goes. Mrs. King said she loves to play cards but does not at all now because she does not like the people in her building, noting, "They're all old ladies. They get up at five in the morning and they go to bed at seven." She also complains that they are too gossipy and she does not go for that. She does associate occasionally with her 76-year-old mentally retarded neighbor, about whom she says, "She will go to the store for me. Lots of times in the morning, the homemaker comes but she used to only come three days a week until they put me on five, so on the weekends, when the homemaker doesn't come, she comes in and gets my coffee and toast or whatever and she will pick up things from the store for me."

When she came home from the hospital after her last severe fall, she had a county homemaker five days a week initially and thereafter three days, but the arrangement did not last long. Mrs. King said, "The social worker came to visit me and I got a letter two days later that I was back on five days." Mrs. King also gets meals-on-wheels. She confided, "There's a lady down the hall that pays $13 a week, and she tells me she can hardly even eat them they are so bad. But I take the fruit, and I take the juice, and sometimes the milk and my neighbor takes the sandwich because I like to have my own sandwich. We get a hot lunch and they bring it hot. It might be delicious, but just the look of it turns me right off. I mean we weren't rich people, my family or anything, but we had good substantial meals and I'm used to that, I guess.

"I have a girlfriend that comes by once a week, She cooks my dinner, well she usually brings my dinner from her dinner and then she cooks a meal here for the next day" [on the weekends when there is no meals-on-wheels]. This is a friend Mrs. King has known all of her life since her childhood in South Philadelphia. "We always said we were relatives, but we weren't. My mother and her mother were girlfriends, and we were both delivered around the same time. And we never parted friendship. Now I have another friend that lives in Florida, and it's the same with her. We were little girls together, and it was the three of us then. Now every year, whatever it is, if it's Valentine's Day or even George Washington's Day, she sends me a check for $10 or $15. Then at Christmas, she sends me $25. And we write back and forth. I don't like that because she didn't have no picnic either. She's retired now but still and all could use all those fifteens and tens, but she didn't want to hear about it."

In spite of a life of struggle with health, family, and financial problems, another constant is Mrs. King's ability to reach out to others for support.

She can be both pleasant and assertive. She has a homemaker who does her laundry and housecleaning. Her neighbor or her eldest son does her shopping. She noted, "My Social Security check goes to him, which is great, because when I was in the hospital this apartment was robbed. [This, it turns out, was a common complaint among the frail elders we interviewed: burglary during hospital stays.] I had saved up. It was my birthday and I saved all my money, the orthopedic shoes cost $148, and I had saved $148. Of course, I was unconscious when they took me out of here and so I sent my oldest son and said, "Go back and check my wallet. Nothing."

She complains that her special shoes now cost $325. Her present shoes are now a year old. Her shoe salesman has moved from a lower-middle-class shopping area to a more "well-heeled" [pun intended] suburb. She noted, "And I said to myself, well, he went out there with the upper class and raised the price of shoes, and that's more than double in a year."

She has always needed special shoes, but could not always get them because of the prohibitive price, and she just manages to get by nowadays. Her son cashes her Social Security check for her and pays her rent and other bills out of it. Then he gives her whatever is left. "I pay $350 rent and I get $488 in Social Security, so I have about $80 a month to buy things with food stamps—you can only buy things you eat with food stamps—and soap and toilet tissue, you got to buy all that, so the money doesn't last long."

In this chapter we have seen aspects of lives that emphasize continuity, either situationally through chronic illness or thematically through the organization of biographic materials around certain key identity issues. The lives we have discussed are very different and means of creating continuity were varied. We turn next to a related issue.

6

The Effect of Life History on Individual Choice: Discontinuity

In the previous chapter we saw how bits and pieces of lives as themes, roles, attitudes, and other elements of symbolic connecting tissue have been used to create a sense of continuity over the life span, despite disruptive circumstances. The significance of these selected forms of continuity has affected the realm of choices (especially residential choice, but other types of choice as well) that informants felt they made and continue to make. In this chapter, we turn to a complementary presentation of material from our interviews that focuses on elements of change and disruption in the life course. Ironically, informants here who have suffered sudden life change struggle with the same sorts of raw symbolic materials to face discontinuity.

The view consequent to these episodes of disruption is one of life without much choice. Yet each informant brings much in the way of symbolic material that has the *potential* to be utilized in the future construction of continuity and the experiential bracketing (delimiting and limiting) of disruption. Such material relies on the two major characteristics of personal symbols: their inherent subjective significance and their malleability. Such symbols also direct choices and help create an environment of independence. In this chapter, again, our technique of presenting our material is in the lengthy case study format, with commentary.

Mr. John Peters (SN)

At age 66, Mr. Peters was quite satisfied with the direction his life was taking. He was generally in good health, was still working part-time, and frequently engaged in pastimes he thoroughly enjoyed. Mr. Peters correctly considers himself intelligent, savvy, sophisticated, and openminded. It is important to him to keep up with current events and social issues. He had always been an avid reader, and his selections spanned an eclectic array of investigative reporting, historical and biographical novels, news magazines, and social commentary. He was proud of his knowledge, his home, his family, and his career.

"I was always able to earn my living. I never had any fear of going on welfare, was never unemployed for any length of time. I had the privilege and the opportunity of working. And I didn't have to change jobs.

"The last eight years of my working career were at K-Mart. Before that I did clerical work at Foodfair Stores. The old Pantry Pride. Do you remember the Pantry Pride stores? They closed in '79. Before that I was in the service. I stayed in the service 16 years. I liked the security of it. Then I got tired of the moving around too often. My first job was as a page at the Free Library when I got out of high school. I stayed there from the time I got out of high school until I got drafted. That probably only served to reinforce my love of books.

"I was happy to be drafted. To get out and see other worlds." The air force took him to a post in wartime Guam, barracks in occupied Germany, and various stateside posts. His mother's home in Philadelphia remained a central location for him. It was always home, always a place to return to. Upon leaving the air force he returned to his mother's house and has been there ever since.

Mr. Peters moved into his present home at the age of 17, with his mother and younger brother. He said, "For the first 17 years of my life I lived in Virginia. My father died when I was about 12, then my mother brought my brother and I here. Her family lived in Delaware County [suburban Philadelphia].

"My mother was the little immigrant girl. Now, there was a woman I admire. More as I grow older than I did when I was younger. She was quite young, eight or nine, when her mother died. Her father was already here in America. She went to school three years in Europe. Then she started shuffling from grandparents to aunt, to strangers, I suppose. Foster homes they would be called today. Here in America she never went to school. But she picked up reading and writing like I picked up the typewriter. And I was at one time regarded as 'the best hunt and pecker in Philadelphia.' She was an avid reader, and she wrote phonetically so her spelling was never very good.

"In my Papa's time she was never regarded as being able to do a lot of things. Like we had a mantle clock and she wasn't allowed to wind it. And, a refrigerator . . . she was never allowed to oil it. She never had to order the coal, do any of the grocery shopping. He died. She had to take over. She had to wind the clock, and oil the refrigerator, order the coal, and pay the bills. And she did it. She decided to sell the house in Virginia.

She came up to Philadelphia and bought this one. I think about it now, years later, and you know, she had a tremendous amount of spunk. I like her spunk."

Mr. Peters expresses regard for his mother in many ways. He has maintained and cherished many of his mother's possessions. He likes to think of them as heirlooms, regardless of their lack of monetary value. Fifteen years after her death, the house is still decorated as she had it. When asked how he would structure his own autobiography if he were to write one, he answered that he would want to write a book similar to *I Remember Mama* or *Cheaper by the Dozen*, both stories featuring strong, admirable mothers facing great hardship.

Although fewer, Mr. Peters's memories of his father were also fond ones. He spoke with high regard for his father. His father was a graduate of the University of Pennsylvania ("one of the nation's best") and he admired his education. In fact, one of Mr. Peters's regrets is that he was never able to continue his own formal education. It was his father who instilled in him a love of books. "I remember him bringing me a copy of *David Copperfield*. It scared me, it was over a thousand pages. I thought, This is gonna take me all summer. Darn near did, as I remember. My father would bring me books home from the library that were probably too old for me. But I hate to start a book and not finish it. Then when he was sick I used to read to him. And his selections, I am sure they were more adult than what I would have read by choice."

When Mr. Peters turned 65, partial retirement was the ideal arrangement. It allowed him to continue his work, which had always been central in his life, while giving him more time to enjoy his home, Philadelphia, and his reading. "I worked full-time, until my 65th birthday, then I switched to part-time at the same place. As a retiree I was permitted to work 18 hours a week as a retiree. Which I did. I worked 6 hours a day, 3 days a week. That I really loved, because it gave me more time to take care of my home, to do my shopping. I didn't have to leave for work in the dark, I got home before dark. I had time after work if I wanted to sit in the park with a pretzel and feed the pigeons. I've always been a great walker, and great window shopper."

Mr. Peters's immediate neighborhood rarely enters into his reminiscing. His job took him downtown to Center City and that is where he would spend most of his time. Hence, the accelerating deterioration of his neighborhood was not a major concern of his. As he noted, "I ceased to interact in the neighborhood years ago. I could amuse myself in Center City for hours on end without necessarily spending a great deal of money. I didn't have to go to a movie, I enjoyed looking at the marquis on the outside. So much has been done in the Penn's Landing area, and Society

Hill. I love the area around Elfreth's Alley, Delancey Street. I am a history buff, as well as a lover of books. And I consider Philadelphia very historical. I could spend hours in the museums."

Unfortunately Mr. Peters's comfortable semiretirement was interrupted only a year after it began. "I was having awful pain. I thought, I thought, I felt like I was dragging my right leg. And I went to the doctor and he referred me to a specialist. They told me I needed a vascular bypass. After he performed it, he told me my leg was full of plaque and he'd have to take it off." So they did. His right leg was removed from the thigh.

"If he had told me of the risks, the possible risks of bypass, of vascular bypass I wouldn't have let him do it. I wouldn't want anything to do with him anymore. He misled me. I don't know. In the course of time I guess the progression would have made me disabled. But I don't know how long it would have taken. The quality of life has deteriorated very badly for me on this account.

"I'm rebellious of the fact that I brought it on so abruptly. Maybe it would've come eventually but it would have been a gradual decline. This way was like I fell off a cliff. The change in my life happened abruptly, and it seems that abruptly I went from middle age to old age. It caused a major adjustment in my life, that I'll never be able to go back to the way I was before."

The main thing about Mr. Peters, in a way, is that he resents having to adapt to his circumstances. It is clear that he eventually will and at his own pace. But the profound unfairness of his infirmity and the uncertainty about the future underlies much of his thought about himself and his situation.

In the telling of his life story, Mr. Peters consistently uses his amputation as a temporal reference point: Incidents occurred either "before" or "since" his hospital stay.

"The activities that I enjoyed, like walking, for example. I'll never be able to walk as well. I couldn't get, I couldn't go out here to the corner and get a bus and go down to Broad and Chestnut, and walk down to Penn's Landing, and then back out to 19th Street. I was a good walker. To go for a long walk, from here to City Hall and back, that would be a great treat.

"Not being able to go out and catch a bus, and go in town, and do my running around, my independence has been curtailed. Although I haven't walked in the neighborhood in years. I enjoyed going out to the corner here. There is a bus stop. And going into Center City."

Mr. Peters has experienced a drastic and rapid change in life-style. Now homebound, he relies on his younger brother to run errands for him and do his grocery shopping. He has a homemaker who does the laundry and light housekeeping twice a week, someone from the church visits about once a month, and a telephone reassurance program calls daily. On weekdays his midday meal is provided by a local senior center. He pays his bills, banks, and buys postage stamps through the mail. Much more of his time is spent reading and watching television. Aside from his brother and the formal service providers, the only other person who comes into his home is a young man he met while still working, who visits monthly and watches TV, or plays chess, a new pastime, with him. But he also admits that many days he simply "sits quietly and waits for the lunch truck."

When asked how he spends a bad day, Mr. Peters said, "That's when I would be on what I call 'death watch.' My friends say I shouldn't use that expression, I admit, but I do. That means just lying here waiting, waiting. Primarily I feel I should enjoy each day here in my home, because just as my leg has been taken away from me, things will sooner or later, one thing at a time be taken away from me. So, I better enjoy it while I've got it. And I do try to do that.

"I wish that I had the means of making a few dollars. A reason that I would have to get up to be on the job. That would be a routine. See, that was the routine that I was accustomed to for many years. I can't adjust. I find it difficult to adjust to a fully retired state. I used to think it would be great to be a homemaker, but I can't. I would have difficulties washing windows or hanging curtains."

Physical changes had to be made in his home to accommodate his disability. Fortunately the local aging assistance office including a senior housing repair service took care of some of these. "If my disability had warranted it, they would have put a bathroom in for me on the first floor. They came here and then another two people came here from their home repair program. Anyhow, they sent a cleaning crew, who housecleaned the downstairs for me. They put up that second rail on the stairs. Gave me a new back door. I've gotten so many benefits that I didn't know existed.

"Before I even heard about these opportunities, I had gotten a bathtub bench and a hand-held shower. Before I came out of the hospital my brother volunteered, and I went along with the idea, that he would move my bed downstairs. And he did a real nice job. He put the dining room table in here. And since then I asked him to bring a chest of drawers down from upstairs."

The changes and compromises Mr. Peters has been forced to make were unwelcome and resisted, yet sadly they are unavoidable and irreversible. Although Mr. Peters still faces daunting obstacles, he has made considerable progress in this first year of his disability.

When Mr. Peters first came out of the hospital he was not able to get up the stairs to the bathroom. "I had to use a bedside commode at that time and I got washed in the kitchen. Now I go upstairs. It was about six weeks. The therapist showed me the safest way to go up. You go backwards one step at a time. I'm conscious of the fact that I am alone. And, if I fell I could break a leg, or end up in a body cast even. I think of the worst things, so I go out of my way to be careful."

When he was able to go up the stairs and no longer needed the bedside commode, he was anxious to move it out to his shed. "I was glad to have it out of my sight. It made me feel blue to see it there in the bedroom when I didn't have to use it anymore, and was happy not to use it. If my condition deteriorated I'm sure someone would bring it in. Or, I could even drag it in myself. It isn't heavy.

"I used to be such a perfectionist. And I only realized last Sunday, how much I have slipped from that level. Because the clocks went ahead an hour. In previous years I would have turned on a radio signal, turned the television on, gone to great pains to have the clocks on the time tone. Last Sunday I just turned them an hour ahead. They are about three minutes ahead of what radio time is now. Anything goes anymore.

"At least I did change them. A year ago I waited till my brother came to see me and asked him to change the one on the mantle. And I have a wall clock in the kitchen. But this time I was able to do them all myself. I felt good about myself.

"Something comes to mind like an old artificial Christmas tree, about so high, which I must have bought about 25 years ago. The kind that folds up like an umbrella. At one point I had it in mind to toss it since I've been out of the hospital. But I decided not to. And then when Christmas time came, I set it up on a little table, there between the couch and the chair, brought all the decorations down, decorated it. That gave me satisfaction. It made it look Christmasy. This was something that I previously had. What made me sad was, and what made me hesitate to do it at all was, I said, Nobody was going to see it anyway. But I saw it. My brother came in and I pointed it out to him. I am not sure he would have made any comment on it at all if I hadn't. And a nun came from St. Sebastian's, stopped in a couple days before Christmas and she saw it. And I brought my neighbor in to see it." Mr. Peters claims that this story symbolizes his past year: the throw-out phase, getting rid of the past; his realization near the end of the year that he could still do some things he likes; and his fear that others do not care about his progress.

"I have progressed in a year. If I can continue to progress I think I might even, you know, start wearing a leg. And start trying to walk with a cane. That's why I don't go out. Even at my best I don't think I'll ever feel comfortable going out alone again. I don't really have anyone I can use as a companion. That's one of the reasons that I am housebound. I will never have the abilities I did when I had two good legs. In case I fell in the street. I think it would be difficult for me to get up by myself. I haven't fallen at home for a while. I used to fall when I first came home from the hospital."

Although Mr. Peters has in his own assessment made considerable progress, he continues to be discouraged and is often uncertain as to whether any effort is worth it. He feels that there is no one who really cares or understands. "If they understood how I feel, they would either prod me to 'Get back into life!' as the television commercial says. Doris Day. Have you seen it? She is advertising Depend's undergarments. She says, 'Get back into life!' Or else they would be angry with me for feeling that they don't feel that there is much use in my trying to get back into life. I kind of like that expression: Get back into life!"

When asked if he thought he would "get back into life" he was not at all optimistic. "Not the way I'm going, I doubt it. Putting on my temporary leg. I avoid doing it. It's inconvenient to put on and it's uncomfortable when it is on. So it is a matter of putting off as well as avoiding. With it on, I can walk with the walker. It slows me down. If I'm persistent it might get better. I tend to be a fatalist, I guess. I'm 67. How much time do I have? Think to myself, Would I have the same attitude if I was 40? And I admit I criticize myself for my own bad attitude.

"First of all, I need the incentive to get into the apparatus. Somebody to give a damn about me. I'm sorry if I am being abrupt. But, I'm—perhaps it isn't totally justified, but I get the impression that no one cares. And then, I think I need therapy. I used up all my paid therapy. I need a therapist to make further progress than I made when I had therapy before.

"I'd like to get back into life. I'd like to get out. But I am afraid. Maybe because my mother was widowed when I was 12 years old. We had very limited resources in my teen years. I've always been afraid of going broke. I've always said, I'd rather have something left over to leave when I'm gone than to use it all up and have nothing left and still be here. I think I carry it too far, that I am afraid to spend a dollar. I'm going to retreat into my shell.

"Getting back into life is going to cost me a little money. I am not going to be as mobile ever as I was with two feet. If I wanted to go somewhere I'd be . . . For example, if I went one way by paratransit, which isn't expensive, it's like carfare, the return trip I'd want to come by taxi because I wouldn't want to wait for them to show up to go back. There's my independent streak. And, my transportation costs would increase. Where if I was to sit back and read my book I don't have any transportation costs. Maybe that's not a good example.

"Would I want to live with somebody else? At one time I thought it would be nice if I was invited to my brother's. But, as time goes on, I don't think I would feel any more comfortable there than they'd feel comfortable with me there. That feeling grows stronger.

"I like to be alone. I wouldn't want anyone to be around all the time. More so now that I am getting older than when I was younger. I never traveled in a pack. In fact, I feel lost in a crowd unless they are all strangers. Out in the street, I am perfectly comfortable. But not with a crowd in my home. I'd be much more comfortable with one or two people than I would with ten. I think my brother and I differ that way. He likes to have a lot of people around."

Asked if he is more adamant about living alone now, Mr. Peters answered affirmatively. "Yeah. In fact one of my fears is having to go into a boardinghouse, or a rest home, or a nursing home." He noted, "I went through a give-away, throw-away period when I came home from the hospital. When I got out of the hospital, my brother had it in his head that I should break up house and get into a small apartment. And I went along with it. I went through that phase. It was just over the turn of the year that I told him, I'd made up my mind that I was going to stay in my home as long as I am able. It took me a while to reach that decision. From last April to the end of the year. That's when I committed myself to it. I think, one of the primary things that brought the decision finally to a head, I looked at the news. I am a great one for looking at the television news. And there was a fire in an apartment house in Berlin, there was a fire in an apartment house in Atlanta. And I said, I might be jumping from the frying pan into the fire. I wouldn't be necessarily any safer anywhere else than I am here. And I am comfortable here. I don't want to push the issue.

"When I came out of the hospital, my brother I don't think had been in this house for years. He'd invite me to his home, but he never came here. He doesn't like this street. I think it's racist, but he thinks that the most terrible thing I can do is to continue to live on Sarbane Street.

"I can cope very well here. This distresses my brother. I don't think he thinks that there can be a much worse situation than living on this street here. To tell you the truth I don't live on the street. I live in a house on Sarbane Street, in which I'm very comfortable. I ceased to interact in the neighborhood years ago. I think a lot of people find that hard to understand.

"As long as I can remain in my own home, I have a feeling of independence. But if I lost my home I would lose control over my life, probably. This is my last, this is the last thread I am hanging onto.

"I looked forward to coming back home when I was in the hospital. I will feel bad when I leave this home for the last time. I feel that eventually I will leave it one way or another. I am not sure that anything more will be done than locking the door and walking away from it, which troubles me. It means something to me, but it doesn't mean anything to anybody else."

Given the dramatic health-based discontinuity in Mr. Peter's life, what resources does he hold from which to construct a sense of life continuity that will surround and overcome the profound discontinuity he has experienced? Three candidates suggest themselves.

First, he has had longstanding continuity of identity through his desire to work and to be a part of a work-based situation; through his analytical intelligence that has found an outlet in his love of books and awareness of the world around him; and through his sense of independence, typified through home ownership, however meager, and financial solvency. These are concerns that are likely to direct and bridge his long-term adaptation to his disability.

Second, his participation in certain social categories has sustained him. These include the fact that he was often alone, never married, and living alone for much of his life. Further, his role as family son and brother continue to be played out in ways that are both meaningful and continuous in his life. To the extent that he is able, his newly increased reliance on strangers and outsiders has been controlled by his active interest and involvement in it and by concerns with his financial ability to direct such help. He is in charge.

Finally, the ongoing life structure he has developed will need to be curtailed in certain ways, primarily in his relationship with the world outside the home and through his ability to "get out." However, there is much about his solo life-style and his interests at home, such as reading and radio, that will serve him well in his new circumstances. In a sense, he is preadapted to making something out of the tragic events that have brought discontinuity and uncertainty in his life. He, too, is a likely future advocate for the rights of handicapped elders.

Mrs. Ella Goldberg (SN)

Sitting in her living room, Mrs. Goldberg appears very small. The room is spacious, the ceilings high, the furniture arranged in a way that leaves a lot of open space. But it is enclosed space, it does not extend outside. The shades are never open more than a few inches. The street entrance is covered with permanent notes with instructions for the postman, gasman, and any other would-be visitor or intruder, reducing the chances of any interaction with them. Mrs. Goldberg, neatly dressed in a coordinated outfit with matching shoes, sits in a small folding chair with her back to the street, her legs extended on a low vinyl ottoman, facing the interior of her house.

"I'm withdrawn into myself. I can't talk about myself in general. It's hard to discuss myself, the shock is still in me, still with me. I hardly go out. I only see a few people. It is not that you don't want to talk about yourself, you just can't. Something stops you. I think I know myself well. I just can't talk about it. What do you do with someone like that? What do you do with someone who's let it all build up inside like that?

"It's hard to tell your life consecutively.

"They are all good memories. You can't separate the good from the bad. You can't say this was bad, this was good. They all go together. People don't understand that kind of love. They say, 'I loved my husband too. But you have to get over it.' They don't understand.

"I can't cope anymore. I suffer. My house suffers. The first few years I just stayed up in the front bedroom, came down to open soup for meals. Didn't see anyone. Didn't want to. So it didn't matter that no one came. I was a lonely little person. I lived backward, not forward.

"I was ill for a long time afterwards. I wouldn't say medically ill. And I wouldn't say mentally ill. But I wasn't able to bear what had happened. I don't think I went shopping for years. I ate very little. Got very thin, which bothers me. I'm a very vain person.

"There have been months that I didn't go shopping. I just wonder how I existed. What did I eat in those times? It's a good thing that I like soups and I like cereals. I can't think about—what did I do in the months that I did no shopping at all?

"If I could have moved, I would have. I just laid in bed more than, for quite a long time, just coming down to open soup. It has festered and festered. They tell me I've lost eight pounds. Didn't even watch TV until recently and the only thing I watch is 'Jeopardy.' I don't turn on the radio. If people only thought, they wouldn't say one half of the things they do. They don't understand. They say, 'Why don't you watch TV? Why don't you get out? Why don't you listen to the radio?' I'm withdrawn. I'm lonesome. Sometimes I wonder if it was worth it.

"We were always together. Never separate. For example, this one couple from a part of the family I've disowned. Whenever they traveled, they traveled separately so that if something happened to one, the other would be there for the kids. Not us. We always traveled together. As soon as the plane got ready for takeoff my little finger was entwined in his. If we went down we went together.

"We had our ups and downs, but the love was always there. It was always 'we.' Never 'I.' I read it somewhere, in the Bible maybe. Love him, yes. Respect him, yes. Honor him, yes. But have a life of your own."

Mrs. Goldberg feels abandoned and empty. She had a marriage and a husband that was everything to her and she now feels as though she has been left with nothing. And she wishes she had somehow prepared herself for this.

"Hold on to something for yourself. One never knows when. It's something that you never expect to happen to you. And when it does, you can't cope with it. I soon discovered that I couldn't cope with it and I still haven't been able to yet. That's something nobody could understand. See, it is very personal.

"It's been a long time but I just can't seem to do anything about it." Three years after Mr. Goldberg's death, Mrs. Goldberg is still depressed, still unable to cope. "It's so hard to cope now. Can't think right. Can't live right. Can't do things correctly. It's always for him. Then you say, Oh, there is no one else.

"My mind doesn't rest. It is constantly revolving and involving, I guess. I don't know how you could explain it. Of all the people I know, I seem to be an oddball, because I haven't been able to cope. I really haven't. I was just going, going, going. Going on my nerves. I really collapsed. I couldn't cope. It was too much. I always said for him I would have torn the world apart, which I did. But for myself, I can't do that."

The continuous stream of day-to-day problems, large or small, is very difficult for Mrs. Goldberg to handle. She sees her life as one giant obstacle after another, obstacles orchestrated to get her down. "Every time I start to pick up, I haven't seen it fail yet, something comes along and knocks me right down again. It's such a strange thing. I just don't seem able to hack it.

"I have a problem in my basement. I haven't been down the basement for quite some time and my laundry has piled up. I hesitate to go down there. That's another thing that depresses me [the termites]. So many things come along out of the clear blue. I don't go down there because it makes me nervous."

She has "an absolute fear" of bugs. During the period of interviews, Mrs. Goldberg was having a problem with ants in her kitchen, which she attributed to the uncleanliness of her neighbors. At first she was convinced that she had seen maggots. She moved all of her dishes and cookware out of the kitchen, onto newspapers in the dining room to avoid contamination, and had been washing her dishes upstairs in the bathroom. After spraying for her, and putting out ant traps, I suggested leaving the spray under the sink so that she could spray whenever she saw ants. This was an unwelcome suggestion. She was sickened by the thought of this spray being in her kitchen. Instead, she wrapped it in paper towels and plastic, then put it on the cellar steps. A few hours after my spraying, she scrubbed the area, to avoid her dishes coming into contact with the insecticide. Each week I would help her put the dishes back into the kitchen, but they would be back out the following week.

Despite her attempts to "withdraw," Mrs. Goldberg felt as if both her home and neighborhood were being "invaded." She complained of a lack of privacy, of people trying to look into her home or sitting on her porch steps. The shades of her house were never open.

She was angered and frightened by recent changes in the neighborhood. "I don't talk to anyone around here at all. There isn't anyone around here anymore, since it's changed. The street has changed, the whole neighborhood has changed.

"I'm not able to get out the way I'd like to, so I'm stuck in.

"This one block. It was just like Florida. You'd walk up and down, everybody was out on their porches, and you talked and you talked. It was just great, absolutely. You could be out here all night in the summer till twelve o'clock, nobody was afraid, nobody was worried. And then the changes started. Black people started to come in here. I hadn't even known they were here in this block, they must've been here last year or snuck in the year before. Because at one time the corner house across the street, they never permitted them to move in. Just recently though, not too many years back, the kids had grown up and gone away. There is a new breed here and they just don't bother trying to keep them out. So between them and the league of nations, I've never seen anything like it. It's just unbearable and ungodly. There is nobody to talk to.

"Those that have moved in are, oh. As I said, they don't talk English. Even the young people. I don't understand it. Why don't they talk English? They come to America, young people, youngsters! Maybe, I know they are all under 25, under! Not one of them speaks our language of English. Listen, I'm Jewish and I wouldn't think of going out and speaking in Jewish to outsiders, because I know they wouldn't understand me. But they do it deliberately. You never know what they're talking about. They should be told that if they come here to live in this country, just like we had to learn to speak English, they should learn to speak the language of the country, and not to jabber away. I haven't met one person on this block that has spoken a word of English as I've passed them to go to the store or something. And they're the ones that are taking over America."

Mrs. Goldberg says that she would never be able to move: "This place will take too long to get ready to move. What do I need this place for? But I like it when it's all freshed up and everything is in its place and the sun shines through it. I still say to myself it's still a beautiful home. But it's a lot to cope with. And the neighborhood has changed. The more that move in the more they are chasing everyone who was here before out.

"I have to make a decision about the neighborhood, either you are going to be forced out. I wouldn't like to be. I would just like to be able to think that I could be here all the time. If I could get everything in its place like it was . . .

"When I come in and close my door it's home.

"The main reason we lived here as long as we did. It was a very good neighborhood. My children went to school here, graduated high school. The shopping was perfect. And the bus lines were great. It was big enough for us with the children. It wasn't only a house. It was a home. Actually, I'd hate to leave, in one sense. In another sense if I don't get some of these things taken care of I don't know what I'm gonna do.

"I like this home, it is familiar to me. Some days I come down and I love it, we had it so long. Then other times I look at it when I don't have a place for my things and all, and say, What am I breaking my back for?

"I'm not really satisfied with my house because it's too big to be done properly. And, I'm not able to do what should be done. But I like to come down first thing in the morning. Everything is freshened up from the night before. And hasn't gotten mussed up yet. I like it. It would be good if somebody could take it now. And do what has to be done. It is a very beautiful home. We broke the walls through, we took off the old doors here, and made new windows. We made the archway into the kitchen."

When asked what the best things about living in this home are, her simple response was, "Being together." But Mrs. Goldberg's home also is a constant reminder of her sorrow and her difficulties. "My house is nice, but a mess. It's not like it was, all these accidents and it's marked the ceiling. And the black spots on the stairway, is an elbow against each step going up, not mine. So many reminders. Terrible. Terrible. They're a constant reminder of what was and what couldn't be helped. I get depressed in the back room and middle room because we always used them."

Mrs. Goldberg claimed that all of her problems affect her health and that her depression was "eating away at" her. The thought of the bugs, she noted, sent shooting pains through her stomach. Otherwise fairly healthy, she was weakened by her worries. These problems were "too much for one little stomach. I go to bed early because I am depressed and want to get away from it." There are no longer good days, and on a really bad day, "I feel like sleeping the whole day. When it gets to the point where I just can't go along anymore, I will sit in the middle room upstairs, and stay in there for a couple of hours. Away from the front and away from the back. I'll nod off. It's bad. It makes me feel worse because I don't accomplish anything. The days go. Time goes. And it flies before you know. After a certain age time just flies. I feel it does. It flies, time."

Mrs. Goldberg has not yet sorted through her husband's belongings. The thought of this task overwhelms her. She speaks repeatedly of her inability to "do the things that should have been done," never explicitly naming the task, but referring to it: "If I could do what I wanted to do when I get up in the morning I would feel great. I'd like to get all my things put away that have to be done. And do what should have been done a long time ago. But see, those things are remaining and they have remained. And that nobody has helped. They shouldn't be here. They really shouldn't be here. I realize that it was wrong to keep them. I can't discuss it. Things that should have been taken care of were not taken care of. And there was no one here that could have done it or should have done it. And so it's still undone. And that is a bad thing."

Most topics that came up during the interviews led back to her grief, depression, and dissatisfaction with herself. Even her fondest memories were tainted by her sorrow, or she used a standard by which she negatively assessed her current circumstances. She often compared herself to her mother. "Oh, my mother was a beautiful person. She was fabulous. And so strong. My mother could do anything, anything she put her mind to. I can't do one eighth of what she could and did do . . . They came over. The war pogrom was on at that time, and the army was coming for my father. Mama didn't want him to go into the army, so she went to the docks, and found the captain of a ship. She talked him into enlisting my father to go on the ship. She went and got my father, took him to the ship. The army was after him all this time. And he came to America. One year later, after saving his pennies he brought my mother and she had two children at the time. That was a happy time."

Mr. Goldberg's death not only changed her life, it also changed her. When asked whether or not she felt that she was the same person she was 50 years ago, she quickly responded, stating, "Now that question is an ambiguous question because you're asking a person who is going through a bad time. Of course I couldn't be the same person I was 50 years ago. We were together. I always had a personality, so they said. Now it must be hidden very deep. Every now and then it creeps up, so they claim. I don't know, true or not. But it seems to me at times you unconsciously don't think of things as they have been. You are still together. You don't believe it has happened. Some personality shows. I always had something that my family was jealous of. I was like my Mom. She had personality straight through. I wish I had a little more of my mother's strength in me, because she coped."

The interviews forced her to remember things she had not thought about in years. These memories often surprised her. "I graduated high school. People used to say, 'What'd you go to high school for?' I'd say, 'To be with the boys.' I was something. To be with the boys. I was in all the boys' classes. I was something else. I look back and it can't be me."

These memories often angered her. "I used to have beautiful eyes. I'm very vain. The loss of weight has aged me. That I resent. I've always been vain. I used to do my exercises every night. When I couldn't do that anymore, I got mad.

"I don't do anything. It has gotten the best of me for the time being. I know that it is something I have to conquer. I realize all these things, but until I get some personal things done for myself, it will never be any different for me."

Clearly, her husband's death was experienced as a tremendous injury to self. In many ways, she was dependent on her husband. At the current time, she is depressed and does not want to cope. It is hard for her to face the multiple effects of aging, loss, illness, and eventual death. The social categories she inhabited for years such as wife and mother are now empty for her. Her husband is gone and she feels that her daughter has surpassed her; her son has little to do with her. There is not much left for her. In many ways her home continues to function as the center stage in her little drama of life. The chosen role for her home, to the extent that it has been given the power by her to compel and direct through its space, is to make her its center, to highlight her dramatically to an audience consisting of significant others but largely in her own mind. Likely, the material that will unify her now diminished life is her sense of vanity and self-centrality. This has great valence in her own home environment both as space and as center stage.

III
CHOICE AND SUCCESSFUL AGING:
THE BALANCING ACT

7

The Miniaturization of Satisfaction and Therefore Choice

In this chapter, we make a brief pause in our presentation to define, consider, and expand upon some aspects of the motifs that have been noted so far. The essential area we want to define and educe from our material responds to the question, Given the diminished health and quality of life of our informants, how can environments, worlds, possibilities, or choices appear (at least in many cases) to be so rich or satisfying?

Certainly, this tendency of the elderly in general to be oversatisfied or satisfied with life disproportionately to objective income, quality of housing, and such other factors has been noted by gerontologists.

We are concerned here with what we call the *miniaturization of satisfaction*. By this we mean that, for our impaired informants at least, the realm of those factors that contribute to a sense of well-being or that mitigate difficulties is small, circumspect, and at hand. Decisions about satisfaction are not based in the realm of big choices or possibilities but in the realm of small events.

The miniaturization of satisfaction occurs in a variety of ways. As people age, the realm of possibilities in life, which at one time might have appeared to be relatively open, has now closed. Having made choices about what to do, or having been forced into choices or opportunities by circumstances out of one's own control, the pathways or turns in the life course have been circumscribed and increasingly, it appears, directed by the seeming inevitability of prior events. Any disappointment in "a road not taken" must be offset by satisfaction with one that has been traveled.

Acceptance is a technique that may be utilized once the full extent and personal meaning of the situation—including one's life as a whole—has been made clear and, in particular, the negatives assessed. Acceptance, or the language of acceptance, is the preferred form of cultural reaction to a difficult situation. Unfortunately, resistance is not. Acceptance may come after one has chosen an outcome or some outcome has been dictated for

143

the person by outside agency or circumstance. Acceptance may accompany the realization that choices are now constricted or misshapen. Acceptance is making the best of a situation, despite negatives. Acceptance makes the situation seem as if it has been chosen. Acceptance can be a continual process, appearing to the person as if the choice is presented on a daily basis and rechosen or reaccepted daily.

Attitudes that reflect notions such as What else is there to life? or What choice do I have? may develop in later life. Situations may be faced with resignation or acceptance, or with forms of resistance. Alternatively, some elders may view the path they have taken with joy, noting that they would do it the same if they had to do it over again.

Acceptance operates in the context of two modes of personal agency: through a stance of personal causality (the self-made world) or personal reactivity (the world-made self). These are ideal types; certainly there are mixed shades of these. In the self-made-world scenario, social actors view themselves as having constructed the personal world as is through their own intentionality. Thus choices are seen as made primarily through the fully active agency of self: I came, I saw, I chose, I did. Reactivity, in contrast, incorporates the self as an innocent victim (through illness or accident), as passive to events ("a blade of grass on the wind"; cf. Kaufman, 1981), or as seizing on choices as they present themselves, as if passing life is exhibited on a stage for the eyes to view and to partake of.

Another element in the miniaturization of satisfaction comes about through the act of self-separation or cognitive or social separation. By this we mean the degree of social and cognitive separateness from the world and other people in it that individuals living alone develop and use. This is especially important for people who live alone who must build a daily schedule and set of activities without reference to any others in the household. An example of this is the case, described previously, in which an informant told of the ease and comfort of being at home, in a decrepit home in a bad neighborhood, and separated from life at home from that in the larger neighborhood, which was "nothing" to him. Further, illness and infirmity, with special requirements on energy, time, and behavior, may themselves act to delimit self-separateness further. Through such dynamics of separation, individuals make a choice (or it is made for them) about the certain attitude they will take in relation to outside aspects of the world: the extent to which they will cognitively incorporate them.

This issue is above and beyond the social performance skills a person may have in confronting the world once decisions about it are made, although, of course, the two are related. But, regardless of antecedent and contributory experiences, when persons, say older, infirm, and living alone, turn their back on the world around them (for whatever reasons or circumstances), then this represents a certain type and stance of choice that is profound.

Separation, then, refers to a certain self-definition as within or outside of various experiential domains. A very common instance of this found throughout this account is how informants subjectively discriminate between the world at home and the neighborhood, which is much more alien, separate, and dangerous.

It is also true that the human realms from which one can separate have dynamic and transferential components with the inhabited phenomenological world. For example, to be in a friendship, one must act like a friend and do some of the things that friends typically do. Failure to do so, or doing so at an inappropriate level, will lead to difficulties in maintaining the friendship. Yet such a process is distinctive from the felt degree of separation one experiences in the background aspects of living, such as the feeling of being a part of a community or neighborhood. The degree of separation may best be judged by a purely subjective rating of social closeness, for example, as in our social network inventory, or by subjective claims about the home as a comfortable world apart or as an independent object of care and enjoyment apart from the larger world.

Next in the miniaturization of satisfaction is the intensification of self in selected small areas (cf. Rowles, 1978; Williams, 1988). In this aspect of miniaturization, what the person loses in relating to the outside world is compensated in two ways. First, what is lost is made up by a rich, firm familiarity with the small close world of the personal surround, or domestic intimacy. Second, because of this compensatory shift, domestic intimacy leads to the embodiment of, representation of, or connection with the world of personal experience, biography, choices, and events.

We may refer to the sense of choice that may develop in this context as *the ethos of freedom in the small*. In American culture, freedom is said to be found in wide-open spaces, through individual agency, and in the broad choices about living life that people must make. For older people, the big picture has often been painted in. Yet by means of the miracle of symbolic process, freedom enacted through the ability to make choices about one's daily life—viewed on the broadest scale—can also be operationalized through small-scale decision-making in the home, even ranged around issues of health-based restriction: Today I will do the wash, today I will see my old friend, today I need to visit the doctor. Sensitivity to the positives of such behaviors is ensured through continual contrast to other, worse possibilities. For old, infirm, sick people living alone, it appears as if there is a fundamental conflation of time, space, and being.

Does this mean that there is a lessening of the realm or space of choice? Objectively, the answer is very definitely yes. The path of life has been taken and defined; whether a causal agent or a reactor, some acceptance of this path, and even joy in one's fate, has ensued; a stance of relative separateness has been made; with health problems and with other experiential changes, some intensification of self in a small area has occurred.

Yet from a subjective approach, one has become more choiceful about things that may appear to be essentially important: maintaining the self as it is. Thus, choice devolves to choice within certain realms. The realm of big choices and "true" self-determination, and the political economy underlying their decline in later life, is mystified through the process by which one takes satisfactions said to be equivalent from the realm of small choices and circumscribed self-determination. The have-nots become the haves in a much smaller world.

And choice becomes redefined in performing those actions that typically and essentially maintain the self. For an infirm person to choose to spend the day cleaning, against many odds, is a choice to maintain the self through continuing what were probably old activities as well as dignifying necessities. It is a choice about the personal schedule and personal order, about how to spend time. It is a choice that is said to be denied to the less fortunate: those in institutions.

For these elders, the act of doing not only represents an enactment of choice (the cultural image of choice and independence writ very small) but it is also an enactment of the desire (and choice) not to be a burden. In mainstream American culture, being a burden is perceived as a shameful moral state, a loss of personhood through a loss of enacted individualism and a loss of the ability to make choices. To many, this is the worst one can be, a burden to loved ones. And then there are those with no one to be a burden to.

A significant component of this, too, is the sense of comparability in life-styles. Many of our informants frequently compared themselves to those in nursing homes. This was the widely shared social category of the worst-case scenario, and current lives of relative independence, no matter how meager, fared well in the comparison. These informants viewed the nursing home as the end of the world, as living death; this is a widely shared cultural perception.

Americans thrive on a myth of unlimited independence and choice. Freedom is freedom of choice and freedom of control. The cultural idiom of independence is conceived grandly in terms of broad open spaces, whole lives, long vistas. This grand conceptualization of choice can, in fact, miraculously, be translated—although on a smaller scale—to infirm elders living in impoverished row houses. By and large, these people feel themselves to be maintaining their independence, not being a burden, making choices about their daily life and activities, and comparing themselves favorably with those with less independence and fewer choices.

These are themes and ideas illustrated in the following case.

Ruth B. Hesse (JCK)

Ruth Butler Hesse will be 88 in two months. Although her back is now curved from arthritis, Mrs. Hesse is a stately woman with white hair and striking blue eyes. Of English descent, she had 11 years of schooling and now has an annual income of about $12,000. In her younger years she was married, had two children, then divorced her first husband. Twenty years after her divorce, she married a widower. The house she now lives in and has lived in for the past 46 years was left to her in 1962 when her husband died.

She was one of nine children. Her mother died one day after giving birth to her youngest brother. Mrs. Hesse went to live with her mother's sister and her family. She married the first time when she was 18, and had her daughter two years later and then her son two years after that. She was married for about seven years before she divorced her first husband.

During the 20-year period before her second marriage, she lived with her father's sister and her family. She has lived alone now for 27 years. Her daughter lives in northeast Philadelphia and her son lives in New Jersey, but he goes to Florida in the winter. She says that both children are very good to her. She is an independent, sociable, likable woman who forces herself to keep as active as she can. Mentally, she is still quite alert, involved in her family and community through the base of her home and the telephone.

Mrs. Hesse lives in a lower-middle-class neighborhood of mixed ethnicity in Philadelphia. She was elected a local party committee woman for 3 years, and was a party ward leader for more than 30 years, until the mid-1970s. She also participated in her local school board for more than 10 years.

She receives a small pension, but says she would have received a larger one had she worked longer. She quit her government position because the room in which she worked was so cold in the winter she had to wear a fur coat and boots. Some of the typists used to wear gloves, she said. When she began working she had arthritis in her knees and eventually, with the cold, it got too bad for her to continue.

She is proud of her accomplishments and said, "I am a woman who speaks my mind." She attended the inaugurations of presidents Roosevelt, Kennedy, and Carter. She mentioned several times in the interview that she has lived among "the highest and the lowest." She is also very proud of her organizational skills. She demonstrated how she takes her pills and marks off on a sheet of paper after she takes each. While we were in the kitchen, where we went so she could get me a glass of iced tea, she showed me the six different medicines that she is taking. These were lined up in two rows on her kitchen counter to the left of her sink. Next to the pills were a pencil and a paper on which were written the names of each medicine she was taking, the time each was to be taken, the date, and check marks next to those she had taken thus far that day. She said that she knew how to do this because she used to be a secretary. She also told with glee in her eyes how she had outsmarted some of the other secretaries who were trying to blame her for some of their own filing mistakes. She did this by putting a small mark on all cards she filed so when they tried to tell the boss that she had misfiled, she took out all the cards with her mark on them and demonstrated that she had filed them correctly. The boss ended up hiring her as his private secretary over some of the other "girls" who were there longer because he was so impressed by what she had done.

Once she expressed her independence by saying that she had recently gotten new wall-to-wall carpeting in her breakfast room. Her grandson told her, "'Grandmom, you don't need new carpeting.' I told him that I would get what the hell I pleased. If I wanted new carpeting I would get it. It's my own money." She said this with a smile and a gleam in her eye. She is proud that she can keep herself tidy in spite of the fact that she must usually take a sponge bath using the kitchen sink since she really should not climb the stairs to the bathroom. Luckily, there is a powder room off the kitchen.

Her daughter takes her to the doctors by car when she needs to go. Mrs. Hesse needs help getting down her outside front steps since she cannot do so using her walker and because she fears falling. Two years ago, she fell down the 15 stairs from upstairs to her living room. That time, when she came out of her bathroom, she did not have the hall light on, but normally she does. She remembers bumping her head while trying to find it, but she does not remember falling down the steps. She said, "Thank God. At the time there was a trained nurse who lived next door and she was home. I always said that picture there [a rendering of Jesus holding a lamb, on the wall opposite the stairs], that God held me so tight like that little lamb—that He held me so tight that He saved me." The painting was done for her by a Catholic relative and given to her as a Christmas present one year. "And I look at it and say my prayers and everything to him." The nurse heard her tumbling down and came running.

Mrs. Hesse also pays a neighbor to come in twice a month to clean for her. Between these visits, she dusts for herself. She can no longer do her own laundry, housecleaning, or shopping. With the exception of breakfast, her neighbor Maria prepares her meals for her.

She does not eat lunch, since she has a late breakfast. Maria delivers a hot meal to her around 6:00 each day. She pays Maria or her son five dollars whenever one of them goes to the store for her. No one helps her by providing financial support. Her son and daughter have power of attorney, however. She had only her daughter in this role, but because of her daughter's illness she has changed the designation to both children. Her neighbor Maria cashes Mrs. Hesse's Social Security check for her and pays most of her bills for her at a bank. She gives Maria cash to pay her other bills.

She used to swim and won a cup for swimming in local school competition in 1914. Now, she likes to watch basketball and swimming on television. Until a few years ago she attended church but now she can no longer do so because of her arthritis. However, she continues to pray at home. She plays solitaire, patience, and casino almost every night while she watches TV in the kitchen; television is her principal entertainment.

This past year she had trouble getting out of bed and had to call her son and daughter to help her. It was then that the doctor got her a hospital bed and she moved downstairs. Her son wanted her to convert the downstairs into an apartment but she declined, saying, "Maybe God will be good to me and someday I'll be able to climb the stairs again."

The teenage son of a neighbor does her yard work for her. When I went to visit in late November, he was helping her put up her Christmas decorations and her tree. She pays him a small amount for this. Because of her glaucoma, for which she was treated some five years ago, she still cannot see well enough to crochet or read. She uses a magnifying glass because she cannot see out of the glasses she recently got, but she will be going back to the eye doctor to get them adjusted.

In the past, she dined out every Friday, but she has not been able to do this in two years. She did stay overnight at her daughter's house last Christmas Eve, but that was the only time she had been away for a year. She went to her grandson's for Christmas Eve dinner and to another grandchild's on Christmas Day. She wishes she could go out of town but she has not yet done so. Her son said that he will take her to New Jersey to visit her sister when he returns from Florida. He has a motor home that sleeps eight. She lists as her confidants her daughter, her son, and her neighbor Maria, plus her sister Sara with whom she is in touch by phone. This sister, her sister's husband who is blind, their adopted son, and his wife and children come to visit once a year around Christmas-time. She used to make strawberry-rhubarb pie for them, although she cannot do this any more. Her arthritis prevents her from doing the things she wants. Three years ago she was much better. For the past six months she has not really been able to climb stairs. She uses a standard quadruped walker.

On her bed is a mattress pad that looks like an inverted egg carton. She does not like it much because it makes the bed look wrinkled and she likes everything just so. She gets up several times a night to go to the bathroom. Lately, she has noted, urine drips out before she gets there. Her eye doctor wants her to get laser treatments and to be operated on for glaucoma. She has a magnifying glass near her chair for reading (although she did not mention reading as one of her daily activities or hobbies). She has a cordless phone next to her recliner chair. This phone was a gift from her son. Beneath it on the radiator cover there is also a regular push-button phone. She mentioned too (and I saw it on her bedside table) that she has a big-button push-button phone.

At present she does not receive any formal services but relies on neighbors and family. She does have a social worker from a local in-home services program. She said that about five months ago she had a visiting nurse who took her pressure and checked her and everything was good. When Mrs. Hesse told her doctor that she wanted a geriatric chair, he said that the nurse said that her condition was good. She replied, "Doctor that's three months ago. What are you talking about? How would you like your mother to sit on a toilet seat for three hours, and this is the God's truth, and not get up. I spent three hours on the toilet seat and I couldn't get myself up [because of arthritis] and I just kept praying and praying until I bounced myself up and down and I could get up. And that was a torture." She said that this occurred four or five months ago. "So I have that whatchamacallit [raised toilet seat] out there in the powder room and then I have a commode. I used that at night—then I would empty it myself the next morning. And I kept Lysol in it all the time. Now I get up and I use the walker and I go to the kitchen and go to the bathroom now and that gives me the exercise to walk and improve my legs."

Maria, who lives across the street, prepares her meals and does her food shopping and Maria's son also shops for her and takes her to the doctor's, waits for her, and takes her back when her daughter cannot do so. She pays Maria $60 a month. Maria brings a meal over to her each evening around 6:00, and Mrs. Hesse heats it up for herself in her microwave. Mrs. Hesse also buys produce from a street vendor who comes around. He came once during an interview and Mrs. Hesse sent me home with fruit for my family.

Maria also does her wash for her. "But that is an expense for me, but I'm thankful to God that I have someone like that. And she calls me 'Mom.' I knew her mother and father. She worked at Sears and when she retired two years ago, she felt so lonesome. I think she is 62 or 63 years old. They're Italian people but they're wonderful people and wonderful neighbors."

Mrs. Hesse's physical world has diminished greatly. Her activities, her ability to travel, and her social relations have all been curtailed sharply. Yet they continue diminished or vicariously. Key life activities are still at the center of her personal identity, as is her belief in the power of prayer.

She has been able to piece together a vital support system based on her knowledge of choices available to her in terms of formal social services and informal supports from neighbors and family members. With it, she maintains her independence in a personal world that becomes ever smaller. Her choice to persevere denies the selection of a "what choice do I have?" attitude. Mrs. Hesse views herself as continuing to make active choices in her life and in doing so she is not only able to make choices but she is also able to use the cleverness and personableness with which she is amply endowed.

8

Successful and Unsuccessful Balancing Acts and the Role of the Individual and Community

It is important to note that the case accounts of individuals presented in this book do a great deal to normalize these persons, despite the difficulties they may have. We present their lives as cases or in the language of stories and the very act of that presentation in a format that we are all used to makes these people appear more normal and understandable. Certainly we have, in this narrative style, presented cases that are dramatic, and we have involved ourselves as authors in the storytelling process. However, because we have normalized these people through the act of storytelling we have essentially smoothed and contained the desperation and conflict in which many of our informants lived. Moreover, these people had and used a number of techniques to smooth, for themselves, their own sense of desperation, techniques that are more visible when one sees firsthand the lives they inhabit. Thus the smoothing comes from two ends. It is created in the act of storytelling by authors to readers, and it is also created in part by the informants. Some burden to smooth the desperation is placed on our informants as they present themselves to us—outsiders—using conventional narrative formats and shared experiential norms, in a more coherent light. Some have interpreted the interview as a chance to explain themselves both to others and to themselves.

In this book so far, we have suggested that much is not well in the lives of many of our informants. For some of them, the degree of this is more profound and more affecting than we have conveyed in our writing.

A related thought concerns one pervasive myth of old age: that old age is a great equalizer for all, that everything evens out in the end. This myth (that the coming of old age brings an equalization of social status, talent, and abilities) in our view masks a deeper structural inequality based on wealth, access to resources, and the political economy of choice. The cases we present in this chapter illustrate this issue.

The myth of old age as an equalizer may especially be used by those who are not old. From the midcourse of society there is a form of ageism that tends to level or equalize all elders and socially to squeeze from them aspects of individuality and capability. Society sees "elders" as a group, as representatives of a type, hardly as individuals.

From the elder's perspective, in contrast, the self is often judged on the basis of past accomplishments and present abilities: What did I do? What have I done? What can I still do? And increasingly, What can I do that is new? For many in this study, there was dissonance between self-concept and the status that society had offered them. It is, however, through the comparison between the subjective—How am I?—and some generalized sense of other elders—How are they?—that older people, too, may gain a degree of self-esteem, because there are always people who are worse off in some way, regardless of who or where one is in life. The constant underlying comparison made by many of our informants between wretched independent circumstances and dependency in nursing homes bears witness to this.

Among all elders, no one wants to be a burden to others, be they family, friends, or even agencies of formal support. Unfortunately, some elders have no one with whom to share a burden, even if they should want to. Some infirm elders we interviewed know well how to use systems of formal support, having been initiated into this usage by social workers, by themselves, or by other advocates with patience and perspicacity. Many others do not know how do use this system very well, if at all. These elders must not only be educated and helped to use formal services, but they must also be of such a mind that this opportunity presents itself to them as a favorable choice and not something else that is more negative.

Yet the care system works in part on ignorance and lack of aggressiveness. If all elders were aware of and went after the help to which they were entitled, the system would be fully overwhelmed. As it is now, this system of formal care is largely overwhelmed and serves only some of the most needy, often those with the most effective advocates. The problem is not one brought about by the social workers, case managers and supervisors, and service providers who truly try to help in a world of limited resources; it is a product of a system, a culture, and a materialistic way of thinking in which the needy are simply not provided for. Social workers and their peers are grossly overworked and underpaid and the funding for agencies that employ them is rarely secure from year to year. Indeed, the very existence of agencies and their manner of organization is constantly threatened by funding cutbacks and alterations. There is little in the way of local long-term planning for the needs of frail elders and if plans are considered, funding is so insecure that the plans cannot come to fruition at the time they are needed. This is reflected, for example, in the current crisis in home care and the serious lack of quality nursing home beds for the poor elderly.

In this book, we have seen the great value placed on their homes as places to live by most of the elders we visited. We have examined cases of subjective separation of their homes from the neighborhoods around them by some of these elders. It is clear that, from the perspective of personal experience, home mediates between the personal world and the social world, the world of the larger community.

Our evidence has shown that, within the home, there are a wide number and variety of personal adaptations to home space, given the range of physical illness and frailty experienced by these senior adults. These elders employed successful and unsuccessful balancing acts and trade-offs to stay in their homes and live a good life, or as much of one as possible. We have recognized that any grand vision of choice flies in the face of reality in these circumscribed lives. We have described the possibilities and textures of the realm of small freedoms and small choices, the miniaturization of these within the home, and the distillate of the life course, those life themes and issues that have been worked into life in this small place.

Underlying our text has been a critical concern with the nature of American culture and the burdens it places on the individual, even the individual whose situation is grossly compromised, to provide for personal agency unassisted. And personal agency is increasingly economic and materialistic and the formal solutions increasingly cosmetic.

A further criticism that underlies our concern here is with the political climate and the increasing lack of support for those in need. Indeed, these victims of situations or chance are increasingly targeted in much political discourse as the culprits! (Facile generalizations like "There are too many sick old people to take care of economically" disguise the great complexity of this issue and the staggering social and political forces upon which it is based.) The two final cases we present contrast dramatically aspects of individual agency, even with age and infirmity.

Mrs. Manhart (SN)

Mrs. Manhart immigrated to the United States from Germany with her husband and three children in 1936. Today at 85, she is widowed and lives in a lovely suburban condominium full of family heirlooms, antiques, and art collected through years of world travel. Mrs. Manhart is a very attractive woman. She is tall and slim, always simply but elegantly dressed. She speaks with a very heavy German accent about current events, history, literature, as well as about her life, family, and fears. She is articulate and sincere, and she has no financial worries.

Mrs. Manhart is a diabetic and has broken each of her shoulders and her hip in the last three years. She stated, "Three years ago I had my accident. But I recovered well. Three separate accidents. Once I fell in the street. We were three girls going to a movie, I tripped and broke my shoulder. Then another time I fell and broke my hip. I spent six weeks in the hospital. My sugar went way up. The latest was riding on an escalator. The doctor had told me never to ride on an escalator, but when you are feeling good you don't think. The escalator jerked, I fell and broke my other shoulder." She now has all of her illnesses under control. She has recovered from the broken bones, and keeps her remaining health problems in check with proper care, nutrition, medication and regular doctors visits.

Mrs. Manhart admits, "I am fortunate to be able to afford to pay for the services and conveniences I need." Yet, it is not just her money that has allowed her to create a satisfying life for herself. Mrs. Manhart knows herself well. She knows her strengths and weakness, her needs, and her abilities. There are things she likes about herself and others she dislikes. Because of this, she does not see her life as stagnant. Mrs. Manhart continues to seek opportunities for growth and she continues to grow.

She noted, "I don't have a high opinion of myself. I know others more efficient than me. I'm not a doer. I admire women, and I say women because I can't say about men, that are doers. I have ideas. I have friends who do what I suggest. I only suggest.

"I should maybe improve myself and be a better person, do more things for other people. I'm not one hundred percent satisfied with myself . . . You can work for betterment, but sometimes there is none. You can't fight it. I'm just glad when there is peace among my family."

Mrs. Manhart lives in the suburbs of Philadelphia. She owns a one-bedroom condominium apartment in a low-rise apartment building. After the death of her husband, a physician, some 20 years ago, Mrs. Manhart moved into her condo. She noted, "I needed people around me. I didn't consult my children. They would've been hurt, leaving their father's house. I moved because I needed people around me. I couldn't stay in that big house on my own. So, I moved here. The cruel fact is that I knew two couples here, very nice people, when I moved in. But they died since then. Everyone I know is going. What should I do? When I moved here my son knew a woman here who he thought would be an excellent companion for me. She was very interesting, well informed, interesting to talk to, but she was malicious. Oh, and of course I couldn't care for that big place on my own. It was much too big for me alone. I couldn't care for it without help."

Her building is set back off a rather busy street lined with churches, doctors' offices, and large private homes. There are no supermarkets or other services within walking distance. There is a driveway to the front entrance of the building, where one could be dropped off or picked up.

Moving from a large place to this one bedroom, Mrs. Manhart was forced to decide which items to bring with her. Although at first glance this apartment appears to be decorated in accordance with the dictates of Mrs. Manhart's social class, an inventory of the furniture, artwork, and other items in her home reads like a family chronicle. She values family tradition and history. The first item she showed the interviewer was her husband's desk. Mrs. Manhart bought her husband this desk when they were first married, and he had it in his office for years. Today this imposing piece of furniture dominates Mrs. Manhart's bedroom. One of the family photos on the desk is of her husband sitting at this same desk.

"Everything here is special to me. I gave a lot of things away already. Gave them away with love. Now I see them at my children's. At my daughter's there is a bench from 1700 from my mother-in-law. I gave my daughter a heavy round table from my mother-in-law and now she has it in the bay window in their kitchen. They have a formica top on it, but it doesn't take away from the table, everyone notices that table when they come in.

"I'd gladly pay three times as much for this place. I love this place. Where else could I get all this light and sun in the winter. I love it. The terrace, my geraniums, see them all in the kitchen window blooming. In the summer I move them out here onto the terrace. When looking at these apartments I told the manager not to show me any in the back. They are nice apartments back there but I need the light and to see life.

"There are no difficulties here. If I have a problem I call the maintenance men and they come and take care of it. They even change light bulbs for me. That is the convenience of apartment living. I am fortunate that I can afford it.

"It's my natural environment. And, I like it. I feel comfortable with it. It is a pleasure for instance to reach out and get that book. That's me. I'm happy in my environment. That's me. I hope I can keep it.

"How long can I do it? My only options are to get a companion or go to a nursing home. What can I do? I prefer to stay here. But I will not always have that choice. What can I do?" Mrs. Manhart sees two circumstances that would prevent her from continuing the way she is: if she were to require physical help, and if she could no longer make her own decisions. When asked if she would consider moving in with one of her children she answered, "God Forbid! Financially I wouldn't depend on them. I'd be a burden. No, I'd never do that. The time will come. I think about this all the time. But we don't talk about it. I'm sure my children think about it too. My daughter is 61 herself, they aren't dumb.

"I have a couple of sicknesses. But they are under control. I have a good doctor. I'm on insulin. I take medication for a blood disease, I don't remember the name of it. Overproduction of red blood cells . . . I don't take those things seriously, I can control them. I'm a little handicapped by my joints. I'm afraid of what I will do it if get sick.

"I walk every day. I have to, for my hip. In the cold weather I might only walk for 15 or 20 minutes. Some of the older people in the building walk in the corridors. They do it religiously. I don't like to do that. Then you see people and you stop and talk instead of walking.

"My only worry is that I get a lengthy illness or my mind leaves me. That's not in my hands. I wouldn't go out in the ice and snow. That is my obligation not to jeopardize my health. Not to do anything foolish. I have no control past that."

Today, Mrs. Manhart keeps herself fairly busy with visits from her children, a weekly bridge game, and chores. She does her own laundry and cooking. She has a housekeeper who comes once a week to clean the apartment and take her shopping. "I get up. Make breakfast. Clean up, do any handwash. Take the trash out. Get dressed. I am an early riser. I don't know what for, it is all pretty boring. I'll go out if it is nice out. Go to lunch, brunch, social stuff. Once a week I go to the market. In the evening I only go out in the building. Sometimes on Saturday I'll go to a concert with my son and daughter-in-law, or a Sunday matinee. I do it to get out, it is not fascinating. In the summer I might go to the swimming pool in the building. It's not so good anymore [her life, not the pool].

"I love movies but I wouldn't ask someone to take me. I go when others invite me. I don't like TV. I have a subscription to the Academy of Music. So I often go to the matinee on the weekends.

"I don't eat out often because I love to cook. Everyone thinks I'm crazy, but I still love to cook. When you leave I am going to bake a chocolate cake."

The most limiting factor in Mrs. Manhart's life is the problem of getting reliable transportation. It is this, she notes, that makes her realize that she is old. When asked if she felt old, Mrs. Manhart replied, "In a way, yes. Because I have the handicap that I can't drive. I can't get around. I depend on others. I'd do lots of things, if I drove. I don't have the guts to get out of that shell." Mrs. Manhart usually relies on her son to take her to family gatherings.

Recently, one of her nieces had a baby and invited the family to her suburban home. Mrs. Manhart wanted to go and see the baby, but unfortunately her son was out of town that weekend. Knowing how badly she wanted to go, her son arranged for a limousine to take Mrs. Manhart out to the suburbs and bring her back. Mrs. Manhart admits that she never would have arranged for this herself, it seemed so decadent. But it all went very smoothly, and now that she knows how simple it is, she may do it again. "But the night before I got no sleep. I was so nervous. I get nervous when I have to do something I have never done before."

The difficulty of getting transportation, she said, narrows her social life as much as the death of friends has. She can only accept social invitations if the hostess offers her a ride. She had to change her dentist to one within walking distance to her home.

"My friends now are just acquaintances, we don't confide in each other. You have to be careful It is limiting. My life is becoming more and more the building. They are a nice group, but. . . . There are two women in the building that call everyday to see how I am. It is a very nice gesture but we are not close. I don't get close to people, I'm open but not intimate. I was an only child, I never had any intimate friends. I had school friends but we were never intimate the way others were. Maybe I am afraid of disappointment. I'm reluctant to think so. I only lost one friend, and that was horrible . . . Maybe this is why I never learned to share. Share my food, sure. I mean my feelings, myself."

Mrs. Manhart regrets that she is unable to entertain visitors. "I only have my children. It is a great mistake, but it is too much work. I'd like to correct that. It bothers me that I don't have people over more, but it is too much. I don't mind cooking, it is the setting up and cleaning up afterwards. When my children come on Sundays I use a paper tablecloth, paper napkins, and my five-and-dime dishes. But guests expect linens, good china. So, I have to get out the dishes, iron the tablecloth, launder the napkins . . . What can I do?" She does not trust her maid with her 200-year-old, irreplaceable china. A caterer would be out of the question as the food would not live up to her standards. And having a "low-key lunch" would "go against my grain." She is unwilling to compromise her high standards. Recently, Mrs. Manhart solved this dilemma by inviting her friends to lunch at the country club, but she cannot do that too often.

This is the case of a woman whose life used to be huge. She had money, education, family; she traveled and had diverse interests and activities. Since her husband's death, she has experienced a move to a smaller residence with a large number of amenities at hand that she is able to purchase; she has had increasing health problems; she has experienced a shrinking social network and the deaths of friends and, as well, reduced mobility. Given these changes, she has managed to continue in many areas primarily because she has the intelligence and desire to do so, and the resources that enable her to continue. In her account, she has presented her life today as varied and diverse, as well as acknowledging recent changes that have made her world somewhat smaller. In many ways, despite her health problems and the fact that she lives alone, this is one profile of successful aging in which the aging person has retained what she could and substituted new interests and activities for many of those she could no longer sustain. Interestingly, this has taken place in a rather nondescript suburb in a large building with little seeming personality, although clearly, to insiders, this is not the case. Significantly, as an individual, she had the resources to do this.

Mrs. Helga Dreiser (JCK)

When considering those of our vulnerable elders who are having the most difficulty balancing the choices and adaptations necessitated by living alone, deteriorating health, and the aging process, Mrs. Helga Dreiser comes quickly to mind. As early as our initial phone contact, her despair and decreasing ability or desire to cope with life's problems seemed evident.

In reality, like many of the vulnerable senior adults we interviewed, she has had to cope with numerous disappointments throughout her life, in particular, her divorce from her first husband, the midlife deaths of the two sons from her first marriage, and a second unhappy marriage. With the second husband, she bore a daughter. She is widowed from her second husband. At the time of his death she was at the shore. She went there during the summer and he came to visit on weekends. His car went off the road when he was trying to drive himself to the hospital. She thinks he had a stroke. Death and disappointment have been regular visitors to her life. And Mrs. Dreiser hopes that when she dies it will be fast like her husband's death.

Her daughter was the joy of her life until four months ago when, in her mother's words, she "deserted" her by moving unexpectedly to California with her husband and their children. The move hurt Mrs. Dreiser so much that she cannot bring herself to forgive her daughter and has cut off any communication with her. Speaking about her daughter, Mrs. Dreiser said, "She wouldn't call me. She'd be afraid to call me." When her daughter lived in northeast Philadelphia, she used to take Mrs. Dreiser shopping at a local department store where she had a charge card. Mrs. Dreiser explained, "But she had a car and she used to take me. But now I don't get out anymore. I couldn't get anywhere much then and I'd always feel terrible about calling her to take me somewhere because I always thought I was butting in." Mrs. Dreiser went on to say that she used to stay overnight at her daughter's house occasionally, "Like when her babies would be sick I would, I was up there a week already. But I didn't butt in that much because they were always arguing over money."

When asked why her daughter moved to California, Mrs. Dreiser explained, "It was not her idea but she didn't like her neighborhood anymore. There was Hispanics coming in and the colored were already there and there was Jewish there and it was getting all flavors. And she didn't like it for the girls. So how it happened: His mother took a heart attack and she had a bypass or a double bypass done and she took a stroke I guess when she was on the table. So of course he rushed out, you know."

JK: He's from California?

HD: Yes, that's not his right mother, but he found his right mother, too.

JK: So he went out because his mother took sick and he just decided to stay on?

HD: Oh, well, so she says. I got word through a fellow, see my son-in-law is in Alcoholics Anonymous with this fellow that brings me my oil. They were buddies. Now he [this fellow] has a mother that has multiple sclerosis and everybody is out of the house except him. And he stays with his mother so, through him, I hear a little bit. I never ask, but [I hear only] if he tells me something. He was here [her son-in-law] to sell the house and he called once but I said "I have nothing to say to you, really." And I just hung up and they [her son-in-law and daughter] were tricky dicks. They were mean about it. Who would leave a sick, 76-year-old mother? My daughter lied. She said, "I'll only be away two months." So, something developed I guess. I imagine his mother has money and he sees dollar signs, you know. They were in a duplex, then they bought a house. I don't know. I don't ever want to see them again.

The last time Mrs. Dreiser saw her daughter was when she drove her to a meeting of a group "that does work for people, poor people." When her daughter told her about going out to California to visit her mother-in-law, Mrs. Dreiser asked her, "What would you do if I ever got real sick?" Her daughter said that she would fly home and bring her mother out to California. Mrs. Dreiser remarked, "Yeah, I would never ride on a plane. They asked me, wanted me out there, but they wanted me under their thumb. I don't want that. I like to do my own thing, to handle my own money."

She said, "I don't think of them no more now. I just think it's terrible."

One of Mrs. Dreiser's way of coping with this most recent disappointment in her life has been to take two Valiums a day. Her doctor fears that she may becoming addicted to Valium, so he has switched her to Prozac. She notes, "This clears your mind, it makes you forget things that bother you, you just feel better."

JK: It relaxes you?

HD: I don't know what it does, but like I don't think of my daughter as much. I was always crying. I don't do that now.

With the exception of her daughter's move to California, Mrs. Dreiser's major preoccupation is what she views as her deteriorating health. She worries about her heart, her dizziness, a pain on the side of her head, her broken tooth, the glaucoma in one eye, the arthritis in her knees, and her angina. She has twice been hospitalized for heart attacks. She also had a coronary artery in her neck operated on in 1981. She has a hiatal hernia and is on medication for high cholesterol. She takes so many different pills that one wonders how she remembers which ones to take when, and in fact she sometimes forgets. The week before our second interview, Mrs. Dreiser's doctor came to her house to prescribe a new antidepressant for her. He refused to renew her Valium prescription and hoped that this new medication would wean her from the Valium. However, she has not started taking it yet because she wants to ask a neighbor who is also taking it what she thinks of it. Mrs. Dreiser is also hesitant to take it because, according to her *Guide to Prescription and Over the Counter Drugs*, which she keeps handy next to her couch, it has a lot of side effects.

When we spoke on the phone before our final meeting, Mrs. Dreiser said that she was feeling sick to her stomach. She thought her new medication was not agreeing with her or she had a touch of the flu. She did not, however, want to cancel our interview. She mentioned that she takes eight pills each morning.

Either because of or in spite of her poor health, her lack of mobility, and her limited social network, Mrs. Dreiser's home of 41 years continues to be very important, in her view, to her well-being. She has lived there alone for the past 12 years. Her home is a three-story corner row house in a working-class, North Philadelphia neighborhood of mixed ethnicity.

Mrs. Dreiser's brick home formerly was a store. It has a storefront entrance facing a four-lane road and a side entrance facing a small one-way street. Only the side entrance is used by Mrs. Dreiser, and she uses the storefront section of her house as a storage area. Upon entering her living room from the side door, one is struck by how much "living" actually goes on in this room. Although there are three bedrooms and a bath on the second floor and three bedrooms and a bath on the third floor, Mrs. Dreiser only goes upstairs to flush the toilets occasionally so that they do not overflow. She fears going upstairs by herself because of her arthritic knees.

In addition to some informal paid help, she receives meals-on-wheels. She is proud of the fact that she heats the meals in a steamer after putting water in a frying pan and a lid on it rather than spend "all that money heating the oven." The meals are delivered frozen on a weekly basis and she keeps them in the freezer section of her refrigerator. Although she complains about many things, Mrs. Dreiser is grateful that she receives these meals. Concerning them she says, "With those dinners I get, they're good, you understand, it makes me eat vegetables which I didn't eat. But then your other things that you need from the store, do you know what you pay for Raisin Bran? Almost three dollars a box."

She has an annual income of slightly more than $6,000, or about $130 a week. This qualifies Mrs. Dreiser for a low-income energy assistance subsidy (maximum qualifying income for a single-person household is $8,970).

The local pharmacy delivers her medicine, but Mrs. Dreiser fears that they are overcharging her. She also feels that she is being taken advantage of because people think she has money. Mrs. Dreiser thinks that because she always has the money to pay for her prescriptions and does not say "Wait until I get my check," a local misconception about her income has ensued. She showed the interviewer a packet of bills from the local pharmacy. As a member of PACE [the Pennsylvania program for aiding seniors with drug bills], her prescriptions should only cost $4 each. But often there is an additional $10 to $20 written in pencil at the bottom of the bill underneath the prescription label and added to her bill. She said she was going to the pharmacy to check about this, but she felt she would probably find it difficult to get there. Mrs. Dreiser is dependent on the drugs they dispense and does not want to cause waves. During one interview she noted that she had called the pharmacy and would walk there to show them the bills sometime soon.

Once while giving a tour of the upstairs, Mrs. Dreiser showed me where the ceiling was falling down in the bedroom because of a leak in a "new" roof, which was put on about 10 years ago. She said that she received $10,000 when her second husband died and made the mistake of paying cash for the roofing. At present, Mrs. Dreiser keeps $300 in a local bank account into which she has automatic deposit of her Social Security check, which totals about $500 each month. She stated with pride that she never goes to the bank to withdraw money for bill paying on the third when everyone else is there. She calls the bank the next day or thereafter to see when it is not too crowded. It was clear that she still took pride in being clever.

Mrs. Dreiser's real living space is her first floor. As one enters during the day, the wooden door is ajar and the screen door is closed but unlocked. Directly ahead are the steps to the upstairs and to the left is the living room. There is a couch along one wall where Mrs. Dreiser spends most of her day. Next to the couch on a TV tray is her collection of prescription medicines. A good portion of her day is consumed by taking medication or reading about them in her *Guide to Prescriptions,* a Readers' Digest publication. There is a trash bag next to the TV tray and nearby a portable sewing machine.

However, she still cares about what other people think of her house and her appearance. Unfortunately, she said, she is too ashamed to have someone come in and clean her house since it is too dirty in her estimation. When asked whether her home was important to her, Mrs. Dreiser said, "It would be important if I could clean this house. I need a man in here to move things. But that all costs money." As to whether her home has taken on new significance for her since she has been sick, Mrs. Dreiser replied, "I don't care about nothing in the house. The only thing I care about now is myself, my health." When asked about the meaning her home had for her, Mrs. Dreiser said, "It's just a dilapidated house that I have to live in because I can't move out of it." She liked her house better when she could take care of it. In fact, she quit work in order to take care of it. She said that her house was a burden because "I can't get nothing fixed. Food has gone up, taxes are high. It needs a lot of work but I can't get it done.

"My bedroom upstairs used to be beautiful. It's a disgrace, from the roof leaking. Part of the wall fell down. It used to be my bedroom." The front bedroom used to be her daughter's when she lived there. "It doesn't interest me because I can't do what I want to do. I used to move refrigerators, couches, tables, do windows, there's nothing I can do.

"I have to live this way unless I sell the house. But that's the only investment I have. I would never want another house. I would just need an apartment. Why would I want another house? I can't keep this one the way I want it. I'd live in one room and a bath. A kitchen and a bath with a roll-out bed. I'd never have anyone live with me. I'm too old. At my age everybody's set in their ways. I don't like people dirtying my stove. I'd rather just stay the way it is. I'm thankful I can take care of myself because I think I would die if I had to have somebody come in here and I couldn't even wash myself. That would be bad. I think that would be, I wouldn't want to live.

"My home was ideal at one time. I appreciate that I got a home and it's paid for. To somebody who's got money, $15,000 would put this in good shape. I can get a loan anytime I want. But how am I going to pay it?

"I can't afford to move. Where would I go? Maybe if I won the lottery? But that won't happen because I don't play it. I can better use the money for food or medicine."

Mrs. Dreiser must make the choice in the near future between staying in her present home or moving. If she can overcome her depressed mood, she may be able to seek the help that she needs. She would probably qualify for homemaker services, which would provide some help for her in cleaning her home. First she must be helped to realize that her home need not be clean before she gets help with her cleaning. One hopes she may eventually come to forgive and understand her daughter's move to California. Although she stated she prefers to live alone because she wants to remain independent, Mrs. Dreiser did hold open the possibility of sharing a place with another woman, preferably in an apartment complex for senior citizens. Her social worker suggested that she might enjoy having a phone buddy, that is, another elderly person who lives alone and might like to talk on the phone even if they could not get out to visit each other.

Unlike many of our frail elders who regardless of their age and health stated that they felt neither old nor frail, Mrs. Dreiser said that, at 76, she did feel old sometimes. Until last year she felt a lot better. Mrs. Dreiser worries about her health and her future death. Now that she refuses to have anything to do with her daughter, she wonders who will bury her.

Both of these informants share the ideal of independent responsible agency, and their ideal has been shaped by the culturally normative predominant sensibility of personhood. Their roads in life have been quite different. Whatever the truth of the matter, we see at least that Mrs. Dreiser has ended up depressed and embittered, and impoverished, in a world of small possibilities. Because of the smallness of her life space and the circumscription of her desires, for the most part her place in life appears to her to be sufficient, although at times she questions it energetically. In contrast, Mrs. Manhart is well-educated and has sufficient income. She has many interests and avenues of possibility despite declining space. In a world in which so much emphasis is placed on the individual and individual agency, both Mrs. Dreiser and Mrs. Manhart are equivalent as individual social agents. They are "created equal." They are both social individuals and legal persons. And both have multiple health problems that limit them. However, by other measures, Mrs. Manhart has the better ending in life because the truth of the matter is that her income enables her to make more of her life and its possibilities, to choose actively among possibilities, to continue actively to retain that which is most meaningful, and further to construct new pathways.

This brings us finally to one important issue, the nature of the community to which these disparate, but socially equal and highly responsible individuals are affixed. Much of the emphasis for well-being among these frail elders is placed on the individual. Some of the cases that we have described show the world of the person and the home to exist in stark contrast to the world of the neighborhood or larger community. Clearly many of these informants no long inhabit communities as they have traditionally been envisioned. Rather, they inhabit a system with component parts, some of which do not fit, connect, or perform well. There is no shared ethos or community in its traditional sense to which to belong.

Government policy on the elderly and communities must seriously begin to face the question of the changing nature of communities and the related question of the load placed on the individual. It is well known that families do help their elders when they can, often at tremendous cost to the quality of their lives. But some 20% of elders have no children! The nature of family life is changing rapidly. And in many settings the community context of family help has degenerated or disappeared. Agencies that help and support elders are grossly overburdened and underfunded despite heroic efforts on their part to do their jobs well. In addressing these issues as part of an updated and informed policy, we must address the following questions: Is our notion of the community or neighborhood a myth? If it is not a myth, what has happened and what is happening to it? Is it beneficial to have a society with such a heavy emphasis on individual agency as it is culturally construed? Are national resources being used wisely to support creatively and with consistency needy elders? Are we as a society willing to allocate the resources adequately to support elders and the communities in which they live?

References

Barer, Barbara, and Johnson, Colleen (1990). A critique of the caregiving literature. *The Gerongologist*, 30: 26–29

Clark, Margaret (1972). Cultural values and dependency in later life. In D. Cowgill and L. Holmes (Eds.), *Aging and modernization*. New York: Appleton-Century Crofts.

Commonwealth Fund (n.d.). *Living alone successfully*. Manuscript.

Crystal, S., and Shea, D. (1990). Cumulative advantage, cumulative disadvantage and inequality along elder people. *The Gerontologist*, 30:437–443.

Fengler, A., Danigelis, N., and Little, V. (1983). Late life satisfaction and household structure: Living with others and living along. *Aging and Society*, 3:357–377.

Hsu, Francis (1961). *Psychological anthropology*. Homewood, IL: Dorsey Press.

Kasper, Judith (1988). *Aging alone: Profiles and projections*. New York: The Commonwealth Fund Commission on Elderly People Living Alone.

Kaufman, Sharon (1981). The cultural components of identity in old age. *Ethos*, 9:51–87.

Kaufman, Sharon (1986). *The ageless self: Sources of meaning in later life*. Madison: University of Wisconsin Press.

Kaufman, Sharon (1988). Stroke rehabilitation and the negotiation of identity. In S. Reinharz and G. Rowles (Eds.), *Qualitative gerontology*. New York: Springer.

Lawton, M. Powell (1980). Environmental change: The older person as initiator and responder. In N. Datan and N. Lohmann (Eds.), *Transitions of aging*. New York: Academic Press.

Lawton, M. Powell, Moss, Miriam, and Kleban, Morton (1984). Marital status, living arrangements and the well-being of older people. *Research on Aging*, 6: 323–345.

Liu, K., Manton, K., and Liu, B. (1985). Home care expenses for the disabled elderly. *Health Care Financing Review*, 7:51–57.

Manton, Kenneth (1988). A longitudinal study of functional change and mortality in the United States. *Journal of Gerontology*, 43:153–161.

Newman, S., and Struyk, R. (1960). Overwhelming odds: Caregiving and the risk of institutionalization. *Journal of Gerontology, Social Sciences*, 45:S173–S183.

Obeyesekere, G. (1981). *Medusa's hair: An essay on personal symbols and religious experience*. Chicago: University of Chicago Press.

Philadelphia Health Management Corporation (1990). *The health of Philadelphia's elderly: Health and social status, utilization and access to services.* Philadelphia: Author.

Rakoff, R. (1977). Ideology in everyday life: The meaning of the house. *Politics and Society,* 7:85–104.

Reschovsky, J., and Newman, S. (1990). Adaptations for independent living by older frail households. *Gerontologists,* 30:543:552.

Rice, Dorothy (1989). The characteristics and health of the elderly, In C. Eisdorfer, D. Kessler, and A. Spector (Eds.), *Caring for the elderly: Reshaping health policy.* Baltimore: Johns Hopkins University Press.

Rowe, John, and Kahn, R. L. (1987). Human aging: Usual and successful. *Science,* July 10:143–149.

Rowles, Graham (1978). *Prisoners of space? Exploring the geographical experiences of older people.* Boulder CO: Westview Press.

Rubinstein, Robert L. (1985) Older people living alone and their social supports. In G. Maddox and M. Lawton (eds). *Annual Review of Gerontology and Geriatrics.* New York: Springer Publishing.

Rubinstein, Robert L. (1989). The home environments of older people: A description of the psychosocial processes linking person to place. *Journal of Gerontology, Social Sciences,* 44:S45–S53.

Rubinstein, Robert L. (1990). The environmental representation of personal themes by older people. *Journal of Aging Studies,* 41:131–148.

Stone, Robin (1987). Caregivers of the frail elderly: A national profile. *Gerontologist,* 27:616–626.

U. S. General Accounting Office (1988). *Long-term care for the elderly: Issues of need, access and cost,* Report to the Chairman, Subcommittee on Health and Long-Term Care, Select Committee on Aging, House of Representatives, Publication GAO/HRD-89-4. Washington DC: GAO.

Williams, Brett (1988). *Upscaling downtown: Stalled gentrification in Washington DC.* Ithaca, NY: Cornell University Press.

Index